S0-BZV-125

THE LEGEND OF
MUHAMMAD
ALI

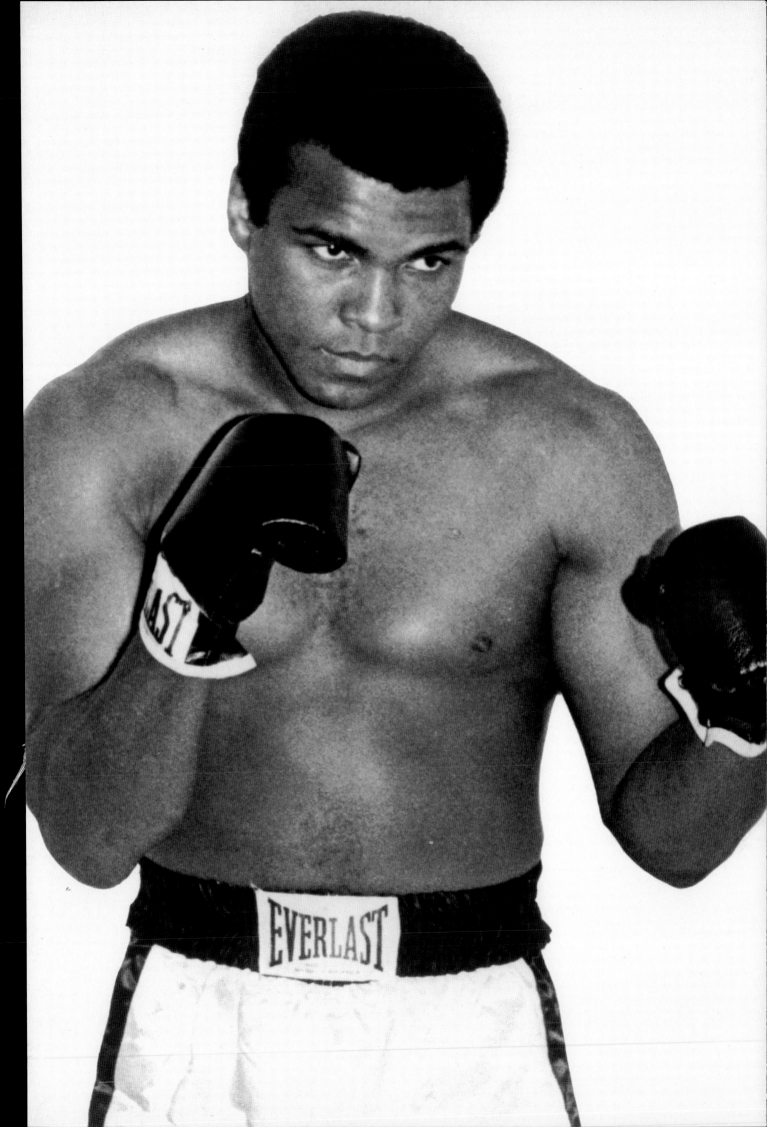

THE LEGEND OF
MUHAMMAD
ALI

IMAGES & MEMORABILIA OF
THE GREATEST BOXER
OF THE 20TH CENTURY

Thomas Hauser & Bart Barry

METRO BOOKS

NEW YORK

Design: Joanna Price and Gabriel Stromberg

Editorial: Dana Youlin and Kjersti Egerdahl

Photo Research: Chris Campbell and Jessica Eskelsen

Production: Leah Finger

The Legend of Muhammad Ali

is produced by becker&mayer!,

Bellevue, Washington.

www.beckermayer.com

Metro Books

122 Fifth Avenue

New York, NY 10011

ISBN:

978-1-4351-2693-0

Printed and bound in China

1 3 5 7 9 10 8 6 4 2

frontispiece CHIN TUCKED, HANDS HIGH, FACE PRETTY: THE GREATEST IN HIS PRIME.
right THE YOUNG ALI IN A QUIET MOMENT.

CONTENTS

MORNING ROADWORK WAS A TIME FOR REFLECTION.

PREFACE

Hundreds of millions of words have been written about Muhammad Ali.

He's the most celebrated athlete of all time.

Ali was a great fighter.

He provoked, enraged, energized, and inspired an entire generation of Americans.

He stood as a beacon of hope for oppressed people everywhere and was loved throughout the world.

One of us lived through Ali's glory years, traveled with him around the globe, and sat beside him on a sofa watching tapes of "The Rumble in the Jungle" and "The Thrilla in Manila." The other has a different vantage point. His memories of Ali begin with the brutal beating that Muhammad absorbed when he came out of retirement to fight Larry Holmes. Hence, his appreciation of Ali comes from a historical perspective.

We've joined our insights and blended our memories to take you, the reader, on a voyage of discovery. This is Muhammad Ali as we know him.

—Thomas Hauser

Bart Barry

2010

★

above MUHAMMAD ALI ALWAYS GAVE OF HIMSELF TO CHILDREN.

CHAPTER ONE

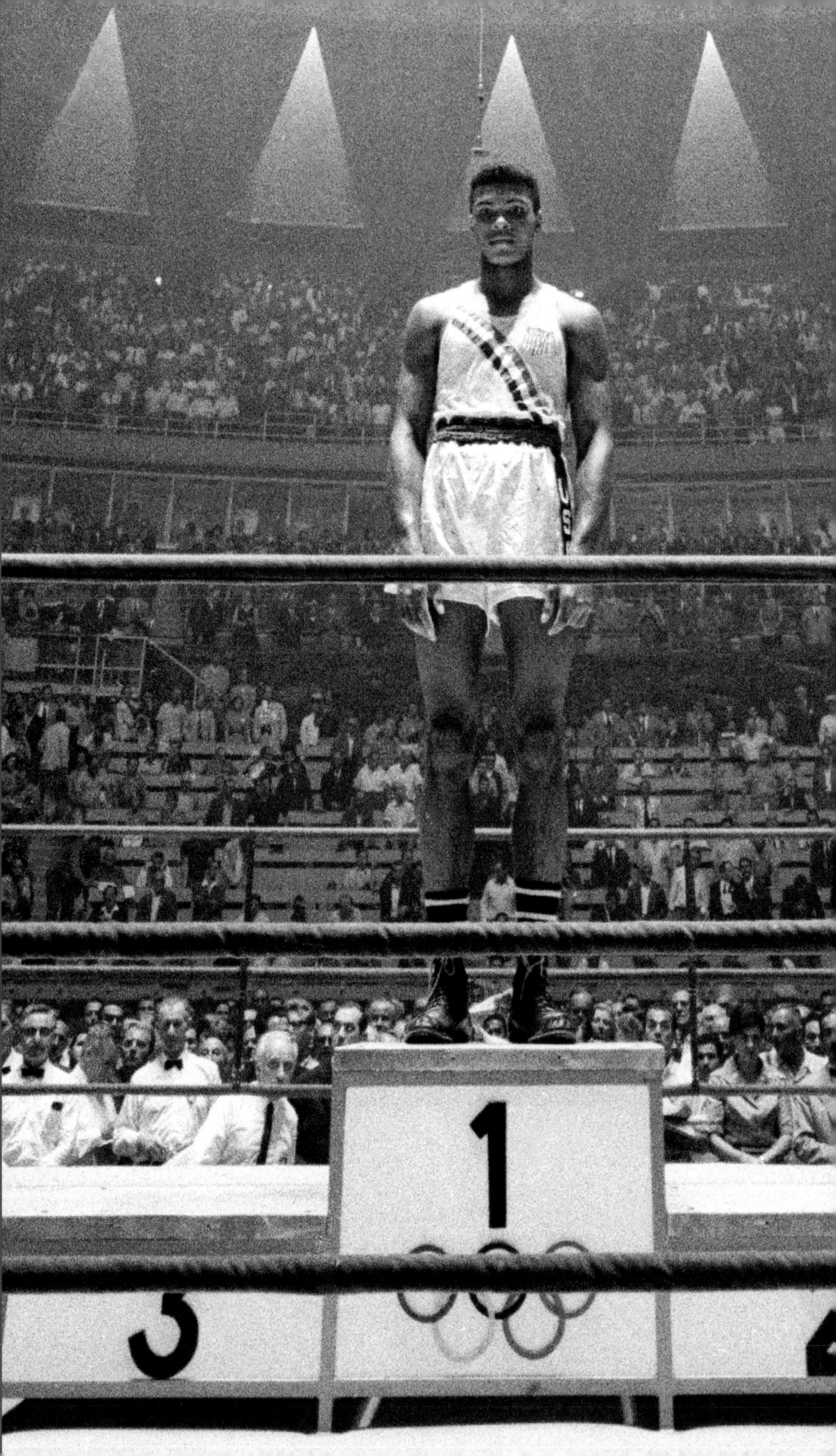

FROM LOUISVILLE TO ROME

"WHEN I FIRST SAW HIM, HIS PANTS WERE UP AT HIS ANKLES AND HIS SPORTS COAT WAS TOO SHORT. BUT IT'S LIKE THE CLOTHING WAS IRRELEVANT BECAUSE HE GLOWED. EVEN THEN, YOU KNEW HE WAS SPECIAL; A NICE, BRIGHT, WARM, WONDERFUL PERSON. IF SOMEONE HAD TOLD ME BACK THEN THAT CASSIUS CLAY WOULD BECOME THE MOST FAMOUS PERSON IN THE WORLD, I NEVER WOULD HAVE BELIEVED THEM. IT JUST DIDN'T SEEM POSSIBLE. BUT LOOK AT HIM NOW."

— Wilbert "Skeeter" McClure, Cassius Clay's roommate and fellow gold medalist in boxing at the 1960 Rome Olympics

Before he was The Greatest, before he was Muhammad Ali, he was Cassius Marcellus Clay Jr.—born in Louisville, Kentucky, on January 17, 1942. His father, Cassius Marcellus Clay Sr., was a frustrated artist who painted billboards and signs for a living. His mother, Odessa Grady Clay, was a devout Baptist who often worked as a household domestic.

opposite CASSIUS MARCELLUS CLAY JR. ON THE VICTORY STAND AFTER WINNING A GOLD MEDAL AT THE 1960 OLYMPICS IN ROME. HIS TRIUMPH MARKED HIM AS THE FINEST 178-POUND AMATEUR BOXER IN THE WORLD.

As a child, Cassius was physically agile. His mother remembered him walking around on tiptoes much of the time. His mind was equally agile, albeit not as directed. She likened it to "the March wind, blowing every which way."

INTRODUCTION TO BOXING

The saga of how Cassius Clay fell into boxing is an engaging part of contemporary sports lore. In 1954, when he was twelve years old, he rode his bicycle to the Columbia Auditorium, where an annual gathering of local black merchants called the Louisville Home Show was underway. After eating his fill of popcorn and candy, he readied to go home, only to find that his bike had been stolen. Infuriated and upset, he reported the theft to a policeman named Joe Martin, who was teaching youngsters to box in a gym beneath the auditorium.

"He was having a fit, half crying," Martin later recalled. "And he was gonna whup whoever stole his bike. I said, 'Well, you better learn how to fight before you start challenging people that you're gonna whup.'"

Kentucky was a "border" state. Growing up, Cassius was spared direct exposure to the lynchings, fire-bombing of black churches, and other acts of violence that ravaged the Deep South. But during his childhood, he was denied access to "whites only" public facilities and oppressed by segregation on a daily basis. That was the world he'd been born into; a world in which American institutions like Major League Baseball and the National Football League were off-limits to black athletes.

It's not difficult to spot who has potential as a fighter when youngsters are in a gym. After teaching them some basics, a trainer puts gloves on them and lets them punch each other in the face. Most turn away, shrink into a standing fetal position, cry, or do all three. Some hit back. A handful, often as a consequence of unpleasant experiences at home or on the streets, show rudiments of the ability to avoid blows. They move artfully away or maneuver inside their attacker's range so the whip of

---

★

above CASSIUS CLAY, AGE TWELVE, IN THE FIRST KNOWN PHOTO OF HIM AS A BOXER. *opposite* THE MORES OF THE AMERICAN SOUTH IN CASSIUS CLAY'S YOUTH INCLUDED SEGREGATED PUBLIC FACILITIES.

CASSIUS CLAY, IN WHITE TRUNKS, WORKS WITH
FELLOW LOUISVILLE AMATEUR JIMMY ELLIS TO DEVELOP
HIS ABDOMINAL MUSCLES BY ABSORBING BLOWS FROM
A MEDICINE BALL.

fists snaps behind them. They understand how to seek sanctuary in the ring.

Those are the fighters.

As a beginner, Clay's most exceptional trait wasn't technique or an innate desire for combat; it was his determination and work ethic. "It was almost impossible to discourage him," Martin reminisced years later. "He was easily the hardest worker of any kid I ever taught."

Many precocious athletes catch the eye of a coach in early adolescence, if not before. The coach tells the child's parents that he sees something special. Teachers and other authority figures are encouraged to treat the child differently. The community protects the athlete and looks away from his shortcomings in other areas. Soon, the child is mature beyond his years on the playing field and less developed in other areas of life.

Cassius Clay journeyed down this well-worn path. Like many gifted athletes, he was a mediocre student. Circumstances and his own remarkable character would elevate him to greatness before his life was half lived. But outside the boxing ring, his adolescence was unremarkable. He barely graduated from Central High School, ranking 376th in a class of 391, and only after dropping out and then re-entering school.

Janet Guerin, a classmate, later recalled, "When he was at school, we thought of him as a nerd. Girls went to the basketball games and the football games as cheerleaders and cheerers. Boxing was different. And he was [doing his roadwork] running along the side of buses. Do you actually want to go out with somebody that chased along the side of a bus? You know; here he comes. He'd wave and call out your name. I remember slinking down in my seat. How embarrassing. My friends at Central never talked about him as somebody they wanted to go out with. I wonder what all those women think now."

AMATEUR GREATNESS

Inside the ring, Clay was special. By age eighteen, he'd won six Kentucky Golden Gloves championships, two National Golden Gloves titles, and two national Amateur Athletic Union crowns. Then he journeyed to Rome as

above THE SPEED BAG WAS CRUCIAL TO CLAY'S DEVELOPMENT AS A FIGHTER.

America's representative in the 178-pound division at the 1960 Olympic Games.

Beautiful of countenance and graceful for his size, Clay arrived in Rome loudly proclaiming the likelihood of his success. Years later, this bold demeanor would be lauded as brilliant self-promotion and a shrewd tactic to demoralize opponents before the opening bell. But Clay's talk was also a mask for the understandable fear

he felt before confronting other men in a boxing ring.

After winning his first three Olympic matches, Clay faced three-time European champion Zbigniew Pietrzykowski of Poland in the gold medal bout. He lost the first round, then settled down and began to score with crisp jabs and fast right hands. The numbers from CompuBox—a computer program later developed to count punches thrown and landed—tell the tale. In

above CASSIUS CLAY DROPS A FOE EN ROUTE TO ONE OF HIS EIGHT GOLDEN GLOVES CHAMPION-SHIPS. *opposite* THE GOLD-MEDAL WINNER IN ACTION AT THE 1960 OLYMPICS IN ROME.

the minds of many. Had he not knocked out George Foreman in the heart of Africa, it's doubtful that he would have become the most recognizable man on the face of the Earth. And had he never shed his shirt, put on gloves, and traded blows with other half-naked men, he might not suffer from Parkinson's syndrome, a debilitation that he confronted unflinchingly while hundreds of millions of people watched him light the Olympic flame at the 1996 Atlanta Olympics.

In the half century since Cassius Marcellus Clay Jr. won an Olympic gold medal in Rome, virtually every segment of American society has found some part of the Muhammad Ali legacy to use as its own. The Nation of Islam used it to win converts. Civil rights leaders used it to uplift a downtrodden people. Black Americans used it to discover new dignity in a country that was slow to accept them. White Americans used it to rebel against their parents, to find new dimensions within themselves, and eventually to impart lessons to their children. Athletes used it for inspiration. And the entire nation used it as part of a process that led to the election of America's first black president in 2008.

But first there was boxing.

round one, Pietrzykowski outlanded Clay 16–11. Cassius turned the tables in round two, outscoring his opponent by a 15–11 margin. By round three, Clay had figured out his opponent. Pietrzykowski, dazed and bloodied, landed nine blows to Clay's twenty-eight.

The Olympic gold medal was the foundation for everything that followed.

Had Cassius Clay not beaten Zbigniew Pietrzykowski in a Roman boxing ring, the world might never have known him. Had he not shocked the world by defeating Sonny Liston four years later, few would have paused at his conversion to Islam. Had he not conquered Joe Frazier twice after losing in their initial encounter, he would be little more than an artifact of the sixties in

---

opposite AMERICA'S 1960 GOLD MEDALISTS: LIGHT-HEAVYWEIGHT CHAMPION CASSIUS CLAY, WITH CAMERA AT THE READY, STANDS BETWEEN LIGHT-MIDDLEWEIGHT CHAMPION WILBERT "SKEETER" MCCLURE (HANDS IN POCKETS) AND MIDDLEWEIGHT CHAMPION EDDIE CROOK.
above THE OFFICIAL BOXING PROGRAM FOR THE 1960 ROME OLYMPICS.

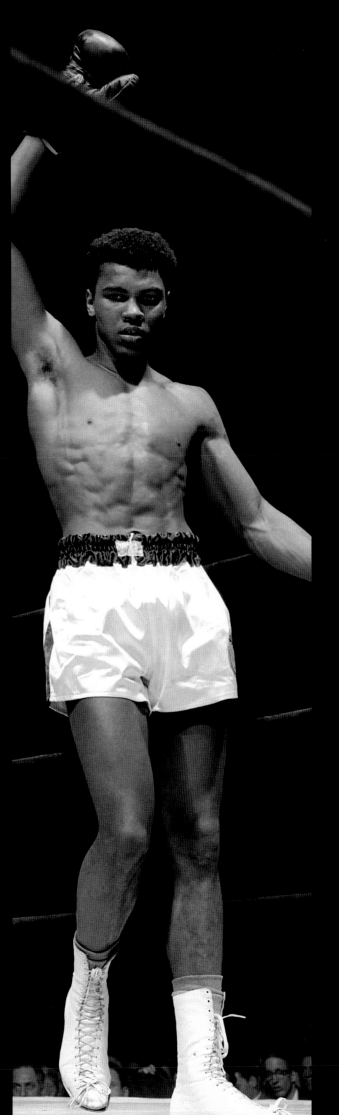

1960 OLYMPICS TICKET

The seventeenth Olympiad in Rome was
Clay's ticket to glory.

PRESS PHOTO

Clay stood head and shoulders above the other
—
medalists in the light-heavyweight division at
the 1960 Olympics.

left CASSIUS CLAY, ARM RAISED IN VIC-
TORY, SAID GOODBYE TO THE AMATEUR
RANKS AFTER ACHIEVING BOXING'S
HIGHEST AMATEUR HONOR IN ROME.
opposite CASSIUS MARCELLUS CLAY JR.
AS A YOUNG PATRIOT READYING TO
REPRESENT HIS COUNTRY IN ROME.

CHAPTER TWO

THE
YOUNG
PRO

"I'M YOUNG; I'M HANDSOME; I'M FAST. I CAN'T POSSIBLY BE BEAT."

— Cassius Clay, 1963

There are many differences between the art of amateur boxing and the craft of professional prizefighting. The weight of the gloves, number of rounds in a fight, duration of each round, and use of headgear vary significantly between the amateur and professional ranks. But no difference is greater or more important than the manner in which fights are scored and won.

An amateur scores points by landing punches on designated areas of his opponent's body in a specific way. The professional tries to hurt his opponent in any fashion that the rules allow.

Outside the ring, prizefighters are often gentle souls. They practice a brutal trade, but are not compromised as moral actors for the cruelty they impose on one another. Indeed, from the slick promoter to the self-interested manager to the calloused beat reporter to sometimes sadistic fans, the fighter is often one of the more decent people in the arena on fight night.

opposite CASSIUS CLAY SHADOWBOXES BENEATH A POSTER FROM THE SET OF *REQUIEM FOR A HEAVYWEIGHT*, ADVERTISING A FICTITIOUS FIGHT AGAINST MOUNTAIN RIVERA.

The fighter's professional obligation, though, is to exploit another man's weakness and inflict pain. He must hurt his opponent, disable his opponent's means of self-defense, and seek to render his opponent unconscious. If the opponent is defenseless and the referee doesn't intervene to save him, the professional fighter is expected to hit him again.

Cassius Clay was a gifted athlete whose job was hurting other men. The obligations of his profession sometimes required him to go beyond the bounds of what otherwise passes as decency in society. That made him a more compelling personage, not less.

TURNING PRO

Clay went pro under the guidance of the Louisville Sponsoring Group, a collection of twelve wealthy Kentuckians who estimated that it would cost between $25,000 and $30,000 to properly launch his career. The two-year contract they signed with him, which included options that could extend it for another four years, gave Clay a $10,000 signing bonus and a modest monthly salary set against future earnings. All expenses, including a trainer's salary, were to be paid by the sponsoring group. The deal was fair for its time.

The Olympic gold medalist made his professional

above **CASSIUS CLAY REVIEWS AN EARLY CONTRACT WITH THE LOUISVILLE SPONSORING GROUP.**

CASSIUS CLAY, BEFORE HE GAINED WHAT'S KNOWN
IN PRIZEFIGHTING AS "MAN STRENGTH" TO BECOME A
HEAVYWEIGHT CONTENDER.

CASSIUS CLAY WITH ANGELO DUNDEE IN MIAMI'S
LEGENDARY FIFTH STREET GYM.

debut at the Freedom Hall State Fairground in Louisville on October 29, 1960. His opponent was Tunney Hunsaker, a veteran of twenty-five fights, whose day job was serving as the police chief in Fayetteville, West Virginia. Clay easily won a six-round decision.

"He was fast as lightning," Hunsaker said afterward. "And he could hit from any position without getting hit."

Less than a month later, after an abortive stay in veteran fighter Archie Moore's training camp in Ramona, California—famously named the Salt Mine—Clay decided that he didn't want to train with Moore and returned to Louisville. In mid-December, he journeyed to the Fifth Street Gym in Miami to begin work under the watchful eye of Angelo Dundee.

Dundee was well versed in the technical aspects of boxing. And he was head and shoulders above most trainers in terms of understanding the psychology of fighters. He had a vision of what each of his boxers needed to do in order to improve. But he never favored the tyrant-subject relationship imposed by some trainers. He had a way of suggesting to Clay that what needed to be done was actually Cassius's idea.

Dundee honed Clay's physical gifts. He also had fun with his fighter. Early in their relationship, Angelo arranged for his charge to spar with former heavyweight champion Ingemar Johansson. Cassius readied for the occasion by singing again and again in the gym, "I'll go dancin' with Johansson; I'll go dancin' with Johansson."

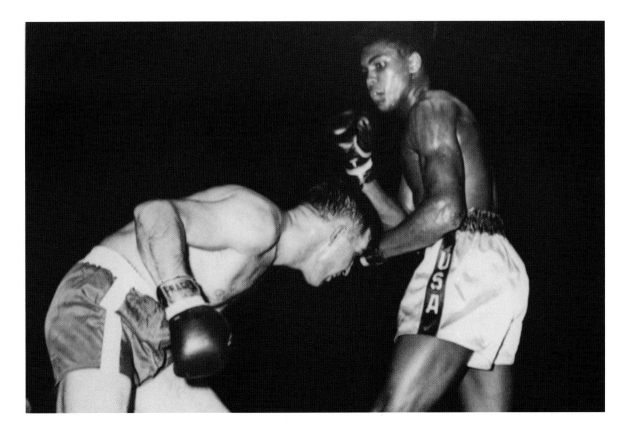

above CLAY CAPITALIZED ON HIS GOLD-MEDAL FAME BY WEARING A PAIR OF USA TRUNKS IN HIS PROFESSIONAL DEBUT AGAINST TUNNEY HUNSAKER.

Publicist Harold Conrad, who was there for the occasion, later recalled, "I said to Angelo, 'What the hell is this?' And Angelo says, 'You ain't seen nothing yet with this crazy bastard.'"

During this time, Clay found himself in a radio studio with a professional wrestler known to the public as Gorgeous George. Cassius listened admiringly as Gorgeous George sought to lure fans to the arena for his next outing by ranting and raving about what he was going to do to his opponent. Then the grappler offered to crawl across the ring and kiss his opponent's feet if he lost.

"All the time," Clay later recalled, "I was saying to myself, 'Man, I want to see this fight. It don't matter if he wins or loses. I want to be there to see what happens.' And the whole place was sold out when Gorgeous George wrestled. There was thousands of people, including me. That's when I decided, I'd never been shy about talking; but if I talked even more, there was no telling how much money people would pay to see me."

As Clay flowered as a self-promoter, others began to notice how much the camera liked him. He was supremely handsome. The smooth lines of his face and its golden sheen made him just right for photographs and, more importantly, for television.

Clay's utterances might have seemed childish when read in the newspaper during the quiet ceremony of

above EVERY TIME CASSIUS CLAY LOOKED IN THE MIRROR AND SAID, "I'M SO PRETTY," HE WAS SAYING "BLACK IS BEAUTIFUL" BEFORE IT BECAME FASHIONABLE OR ACCEPTED.

CLAY WARMS UP IN HIS DRESSING ROOM, PREPARING
TO "DANCE" AS NO HEAVYWEIGHT HAS DONE
BEFORE OR SINCE.

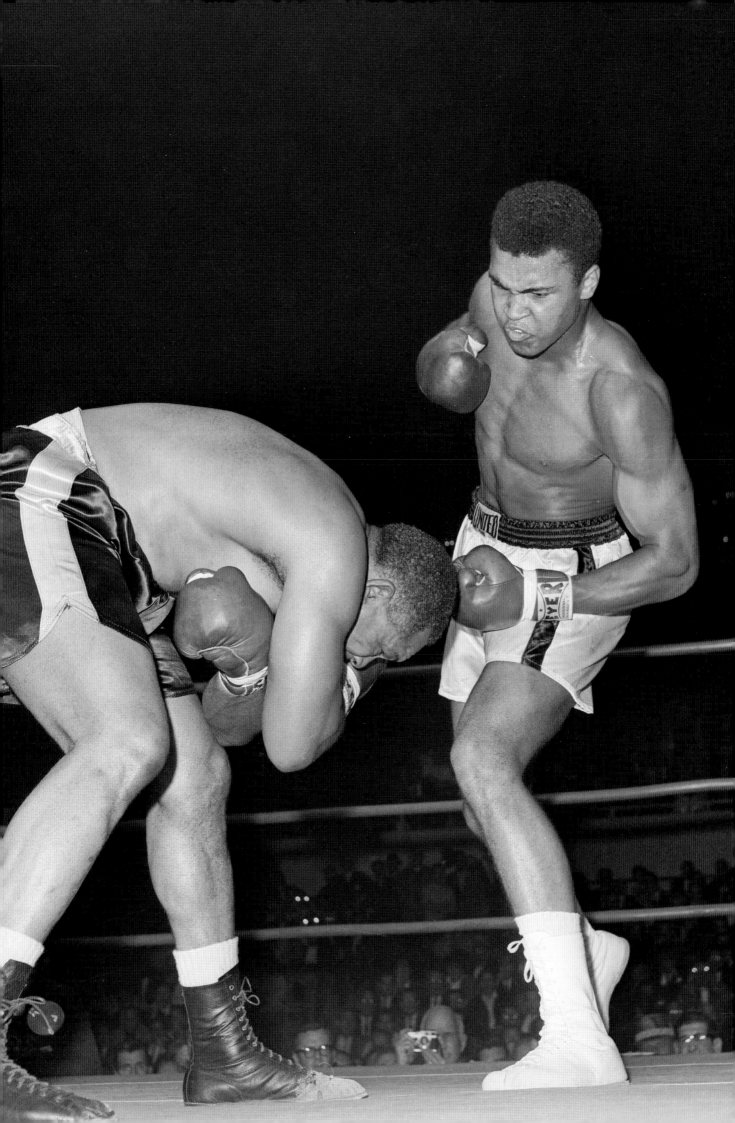

a morning breakfast. But delivered by a wide-eyed, incredibly good-looking young man through the medium of television, they could be mesmerizing. The cadence of his speech, the timbre of his voice, and the joy he took in his own words drew viewers in. He was an entertainer.

CLIMBING THE RANKS

On November 15, 1962, twenty-year-old Cassius Clay fought Archie "The Old Mongoose" Moore. Clay, by then, was undefeated in fifteen professional bouts with twelve knockouts to his credit. Moore was a veteran of 217 fights; the perpetrator of 130 knockouts; and by most accounts, forty-eight years old.

Moore hoped to exploit the technical flaws in Clay's style. Cassius held his hands perilously low. He committed the cardinal sin of pulling his head back from punches rather than moving it to the side or down. When dancing away from an opponent, Clay occasionally swung his right foot behind his left. When a fighter crosses his feet, it can leave him off balance and temporarily vulnerable to his foe.

Clay clinched effectively on the inside insofar as he used his left arm to neutralize his opponent's right. But he sometimes neglected to hold his opponent's left elbow in place with his own right arm. That left the opponent free to throw left hooks.

When Cassius threw a jab, his right glove strayed from its protective position by his right cheek. That meant he was vulnerable to jabs and left hooks coming back.

But because of Clay's preternatural speed, none of those flaws mattered against Moore. After taking a one-sided beating, "The Old Mongoose" was knocked out in the fourth round.

Years later, Moore, one of the great light-heavyweight champions of all time, was asked if the result might have been different had he been in his prime.

"I don't think so," Moore answered. "One never knows for sure. But I believe in my mind and heart that Ali would have beaten Joe Louis. If they'd fought five times, Ali would have won four. I was a pretty good light-heavyweight, but I think Joe Louis would have beaten me."

Victories over Charlie Powell and Doug Jones followed

opposite CLAY'S FOURTH-ROUND KNOCKOUT OF FORTY-EIGHT-YEAR-OLD ARCHIE MOORE IN 1962 WAS THE FIRST BIG NAME ON CASSIUS'S RÉSUMÉ. *above* THE OFFICIAL FIGHT PROGRAM FROM ARCHIE MOORE VERSUS CASSIUS CLAY GAVE TOP BILLING TO MOORE.

Clay's conquest of Moore. Then Cassius journeyed to London to face the British Commonwealth and British heavyweight champion, Henry Cooper.

Fifty-five thousand fans filled Wembley Stadium for the occasion. Cooper was a decided underdog. The most pressing question with regard to the outcome of the bout seemed to be whether Clay would make good on his prediction of a fifth-round knockout.

For three rounds, two minutes, and fifty-five seconds, Cassius toyed with his overmatched foe; hitting him at will and opening deep cuts; easing off each time in anticipation of the fifth round.

Then the unexpected happened. Matching speed with timing, Cooper launched a classic left hook over Clay's low right hand. The blow landed flush on Cassius's jaw, propelling him into the ropes and down onto the canvas.

Clay rose, starry-eyed and on shaky legs. The bell ending the round sounded. Cassius's seconds propped him up and led him to his corner. Moments later, he stood up from his stool as though still trying to beat the referee's count. Smelling salts were held under his nose. When that failed to fully restore his senses, Angelo Dundee pulled at a small tear in the seam of his fighter's glove and brought it to the attention of referee Tommy Little.

Precious seconds passed before it was determined that there were no backup gloves at ringside. The action resumed. Clay's remarkable recuperative powers took over. Two minutes and fifteen seconds into round five, with Cooper bleeding as though his face had been sliced open by a box cutter, the fight was stopped.

"THE BIG UGLY BEAR"

Eight months later, on February 25, 1964, Clay challenged Charles "Sonny" Liston for the heavyweight championship of the world.

Liston was a cold, menacing presence, an ex-convict once employed as a strong-arm man for the mob and now promoted by them. His career had been advanced by Frankie Carbo and Blinky Palermo, both of whom were familiar with the inside of a prison. He'd won and then successfully defended the heavyweight championship by knocking out Floyd Patterson twice; needing slightly more than two minutes to do the job each time. Many in the boxing community thought of him as invulnerable.

above HENRY COOPER TRIED TO EXPLOIT CASSIUS CLAY'S LOW GUARD AND HIGH CHIN.
opposite CHALLENGING SONNY LISTON, ONE OF THE MOST FEARED FIGHTERS OF ALL TIME, CLAY CLOSED THE CHAMPION'S EYES WITH SWIFT, SHARP PUNCHES.

Days before his rematch against Patterson, Liston had been sitting at a Las Vegas craps table, doing poorly with the dice, when Clay appeared on the scene and began to taunt him.

Liston responded with an expletive-laden threat to rip Clay's tongue out of his mouth and shove it up a body cavity if Clay didn't depart in ten seconds.

The count never reached ten.

"That big ugly bear scared me bad," Clay acknowledged later that night.

Clay entered the ring against Liston as a 7–1 underdog. Given an empty alley and no rules to follow, it's likely that the mobbed-up champion would have mauled the challenger, just like the bear of his moniker. But they weren't fighting in an alley. The venue was a padded canvas enclosed within ropes; the battle to be fought in accordance with rules of combat under the supervision of a referee.

"Just before the fight, when the referee was giving us instructions, Liston was giving me that stare," Clay later said. "I won't lie; I was scared. Sonny Liston was one of the greatest fighters of all time. It frightened me, just knowing how hard he hit. But I was there. I didn't have no choice but to go out and fight."

Cassius Clay was on the verge of greatness as a fighter.

Moving gracefully and circling to his left, Clay kept out of range of Liston's blows. When Sonny worked his way inside, Cassius tied him up in a clinch or pushed him off.

The first round passed. The challenger's confidence grew. In round three, Clay opened a gash on Liston's left cheek and raised a bruise beneath the champion's right eye. Then a new act in the drama unfolded. Near the end of round four, Cassius began having trouble with his eyes. It was suspected that a caustic substance—thought to be either a coagulant that one of Liston's cornermen applied to the cut or an astringent that was illegally rubbed on his gloves with evil intent—temporarily blinded the challenger. Years later, cornerman Joe Polino admitted the latter scenario was the cause.

Between rounds, Dundee rinsed his fighter's eyes with a sponge. Then he pushed him out for the fifth stanza. Clay survived the next three minutes by moving, staying out of range, and breaking Liston's rhythm with occasional jabs. Then his eyes cleared and he pounded

★

---

opposite (top) CLAY'S QUICK HANDS MADE LISTON LOOK OLD AND SLOW. *opposite (bottom)* "I SHOOK UP THE WORLD!" NEVER ONE FOR A QUIET CELEBRATION, CASSIUS CLAY LEAPS INTO A CORNER-MAN'S ARMS AFTER BECOMING BOXING'S YOUNGEST HEAVYWEIGHT CHAMPION. *above* THE NEW HEAVYWEIGHT CHAMPION OF THE WORLD PREPARES FOR A POST-FIGHT INTERVIEW WITH COR-NERMAN DREW BUNDINI BROWN AT HIS SIDE.

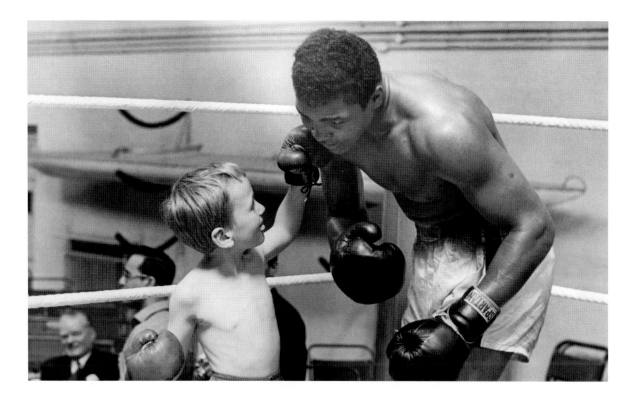

the hell out of the champion. Liston quit on his stool at the end of six rounds.

At age twenty-two, Cassius Marcellus Clay Jr. was the youngest heavyweight champion in history.

It was Clay's twentieth professional fight. Not since 1899, when James Jeffries dethroned Bob Fitzsimmons in his twelfth prizefight, had a fighter won the heavyweight championship with fewer battles on his record.

As the beaten Liston slumped on his stool, Clay raised his arms upward toward the heavens. His feet skimmed back and forth across the canvas with such speed that he appeared to be levitating.

"I am the greatest," he shouted. "I'm the king of the world. I'm pretty. I'm a bad man. I can't be beat. I shook up the world."

Cassius Clay had always delighted in the attention of others. From that night on, he had it. Even as his fame expanded beyond sports, when as Muhammad Ali he would become the most recognizable person on the planet, he never treated his fame as a burden. He would oblige fans with small acts of kindness as often as all of his predecessors put together. He always understood the meaningfulness of a hug, a handshake, an autograph, or a photo of the heavyweight champion standing with his arm around a total stranger who would cherish the memento forever. He wasn't acting pursuant to a marketer's plan. He didn't give of his time to ensure that he could charge more for it later on. He gave of himself from the heart. In due course, that would be fully appreciated by the world. But the journey would be a long one.

★

above CASSIUS CLAY SPARS WITH A FUTURE PROSPECT, DELIGHTING AS HE ALWAYS DID IN THE PRESENCE OF CHILDREN. *opposite* "I'M A BAAAAD MAN!" CLAY STRIKES ONE OF HIS FAMOUS OPEN-MOUTH POSES AFTER DETHRONING LISTON.

CLAY VS. HUNSAKER
PROGRAM

Clay's professional debut against Tunney
Hunsaker was marked by a bare-bones fight
program.

PRESS PHOTO

Clay's February 25, 1964, victory over Sonny
Liston ushered in a new era for boxing and all
of professional sports.

left THE NEW CHAMPION WITH *RING
MAGAZINE'S* CHAMPIONSHIP BELT.
opposite LOOKING MOCK MEAN.

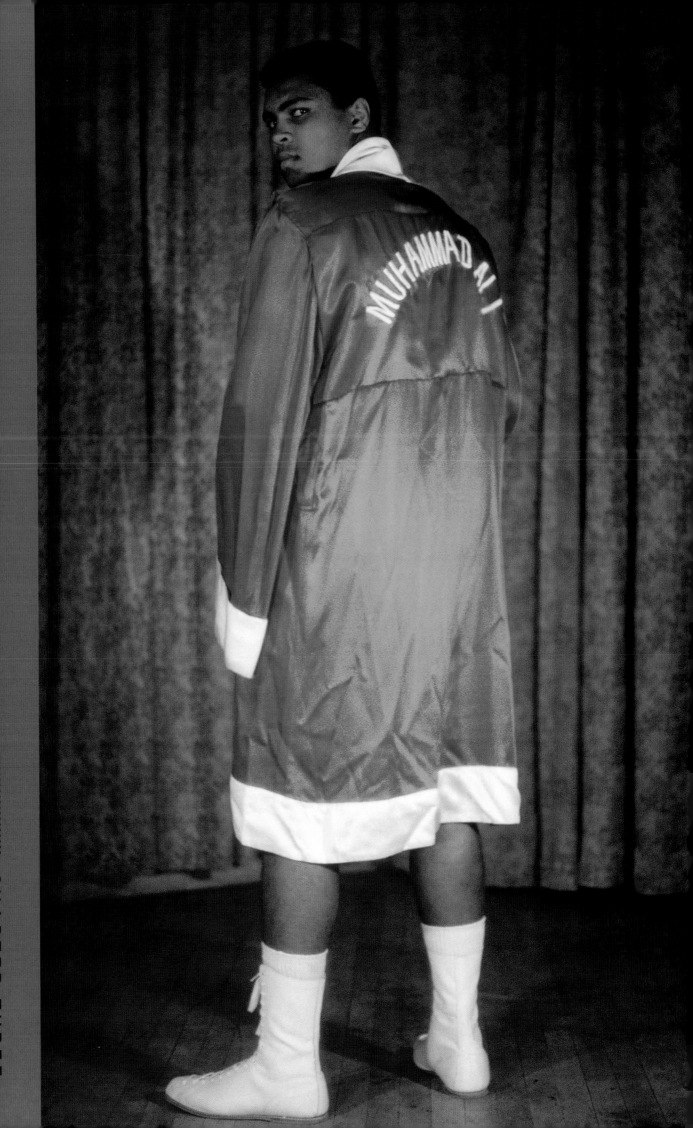

CHAPTER THREE

CASSIUS CLAY BECOMES MUHAMMAD ALI

"CLAY WILL MEAN MORE TO HIS PEOPLE THAN JACKIE ROBINSON, BECAUSE ROBINSON IS THE WHITE MAN'S HERO, BUT CASSIUS IS THE BLACK MAN'S HERO."

— *Malcolm X*

Time extends seamlessly. But decades often have an identity of their own.

The Roaring Twenties in the United States were known for speakeasies, the popularization of spectator sports, and the explosion of mass culture. The 1930s were dominated by the Great Depression; the 1940s by World War II. The 1950s saw a "return to normalcy" and the belief that the American people could accomplish anything that they set their minds to.

The sixties were like no other era: assassinations, the war in Vietnam, the growth of television as an entertainment and news medium, the sexual revolution, recreational drugs, black America rising to assert itself.

Within a three-month span, three events that defined the sixties occurred. On November 22, 1963, John F. Kennedy was assassinated in Dallas. On February 9, 1964, the Beatles made their American debut on *The Ed Sullivan Show*. And on February 25,

opposite THE NEW CHAMPION ANSWERS TO A NEW NAME.

1964, Cassius Clay dethroned Sonny Liston to become heavyweight champion of the world.

Forget the calendar. Those three months were when the sixties began.

THE NATION OF ISLAM

One day after he defeated Sonny Liston, the new champion held a press conference and confirmed that he was no longer a Christian. Asked if he was a "card-carrying member of the Black Muslims," he parried the question by wondering what sort of a card that would be. He added that he believed in Allah and would not want to marry a white woman.

The next day Clay was more direct about his new religious identity. At a second press conference, he told reporters that "Black Muslim" was a term invented by the white media and unveiled himself as a follower of Elijah Muhammad. He then advised those in attendance that the Nation of Islam was not a "hate group," but rather was comprised of the "sweetest people in the world." He also referenced Nation of Islam dogma, explaining, "I don't believe in forced integration. I just want to be happy with my own kind. If I go in somebody's house where I'm not welcome, I'm uncomfortable, so I stay away. I like white people. I like my own people. They can live together without infringing on each other."

Those words, spoken by the heavyweight champion of the world, sent shockwaves across the country.

The Nation of Islam was viewed by the American establishment, black and white, as an ominous subversive

★

above NEWS THAT THE HEAVYWEIGHT CHAMPION OF THE WORLD WAS A "BLACK MUSLIM" PERTURBED MANY AMERICANS. THERE WERE QUESTIONS TO BE ANSWERED, INCLUDING THOSE IN THIS INTERVIEW WITH CBS.

THE NEWLY NAMED MUHAMMAD ALI HOLDS A COPY
OF *MUHAMMAD SPEAKS*, THE NATION OF ISLAM'S WEEKLY
NEWSPAPER.

Former champions Joe Louis and Floyd Patterson spoke for many when they criticized attaching a racial ideology to the heavyweight crown. Lost in the outrage was the fact that portions of this ideology were an uplifting force for many black Americans. In theory, the Nation's ministers taught self-respect, sobriety, abstinence, charity, and self-love.

CASSIUS CLAY'S CONVERSION

Cassius Clay first heard of the teachings of Elijah Muhammad while attending a 1959 Golden Gloves tournament in Chicago. He saw a copy of the Nation of Islam newspaper, *Muhammad Speaks*, but didn't think much about it afterward. Then, while training in Miami in 1961, he met a Nation of Islam convert known as Captain Sam. Soon, he was attending temple services on a regular basis.

Clay's first teacher in the Nation of Islam was a minister named Ishmael Sabakhan. Then a senior cleric named Jeremiah Shabazz took over his tutelage. Those two men taught him the basics of the religion and laid the groundwork for what followed. Finally, Cassius fell under the spell of the religion's best-known and most charismatic minister, Malcolm X, whom he met for the first time at a 1962 rally in Detroit.

organization that preached intolerance. Its teachings differed significantly from Orthodox Islam in many respects.

The Qur'an teaches that life on Earth is in large measure about preparation for the hereafter. Under Nation of Islam doctrine, heaven and hell do not exist. The Qur'an teaches that Muhammad was Allah's final prophet. The Nation of Islam taught that Elijah Muhammad, who founded the religion in 1931, was one of God's prophets. More significantly as far as most Americans were concerned, Islam adheres to the premise that hearts and souls have no color. Nation of Islam ministers preached that white people were devils created by an evil scientist named Mr. Yacub and that, for black Americans, "integration means destruction."

Commentators of all colors dismissed the teachings of the Nation of Islam as "racism for black people."

"My husband accepted Cassius and loved him like a younger brother," Betty Shabazz, Malcolm's widow, later recalled. "He felt his job was to get this young man to believe in himself and stand squarely on both feet with his shoulders back. He felt he could do more and be more."

opposite POPULAR AS EVER IN THE BLACK COMMUNITY, ALI TAKES A WALK IN HARLEM WITH FRIENDS AND SUPPORTERS. *above* MUHAMMAD ALI AT PRAYER AT THE AL-HUSSEIN MOSQUE IN CAIRO, EGYPT.

Malcolm was a frequent presence in Clay's training camp during the weeks leading up to the Liston-Clay fight. He was there, not as an emissary of Elijah Muhammad (who assumed that the challenger would be defeated), but as Cassius's guest.

After Clay defeated Liston, Elijah Muhammad's interest in the young fighter grew. On March 6, 1964, he announced in a radio address to his followers that he'd given the champion a new name.

"This Clay name has no divine meaning," Elijah proclaimed. "I hope he will accept being called by a better name. Muhammad Ali is what I will give him for as long as he believes in Allah and follows me."

THE BACKLASH

America's fondness for its Olympic son was now challenged. He had been a feel-good story. A poor "colored" boy from the South, taught to box by a white policeman and guided through the shark-infested waters of boxing by twelve benevolent white men. At times, his braggadocian outbursts had been irksome: "I'm so pretty. I am the greatest." But he'd been entertaining. This new development was sinister and threatening.

Meanwhile, the Nation of Islam was falling into turmoil. Malcolm X was increasingly troubled by allegations of sexual misconduct and financial impropriety that had been lodged against Elijah Muhammad. After a

★

above MUHAMMAD ALI WITH HIS ARM AROUND ELIJAH MUHAMMAD, FOUNDER OF THE NATION OF ISLAM AND THE MAN WHO GAVE HIM THE NAME HE'D CARRY FOR THE REST OF HIS LIFE. *opposite* ONE CHARISMATIC AGENT OF SOCIAL CHANGE LEANS ON ANOTHER. MUHAMMAD ALI LOOKS OVER HIS SHOULDER AT MALCOLM X.

pilgrimage to Mecca, he returned to question his leader's teachings.

Branding Elijah a "religious fakir," Malcolm declared, "In the past, I have made sweeping indictments of all white people. I will never be guilty of that again as I know now that some white people are truly sincere, that some truly are capable of being brotherly toward a black man. The true Islam has shown me that a blanket indictment of all white people is as wrong as when whites make blanket indictments against blacks."

Elijah Muhammad responded by permanently banishing Malcolm from the Nation of Islam. But his charismatic protégé's voice grew ever louder, and the chasm between the two men widened.

Muhammad Ali was forced to take sides. He chose Elijah and never embraced Malcolm again.

"My father was hurt that Ali didn't speak up on his behalf," Attallah Shabazz, Malcolm's daughter, said years later. "But he understood why and never stopped loving him."

Decades after the fact, Ali would voice regret over distancing himself from Malcolm. It was a decision he made based on what he believed was right at the time. And perhaps an element of fear was involved. A decade later, Ali told journalist Dave Kindred, "I would have gotten out of [the Nation of Islam] a long time ago. But you saw what they did to Malcolm."

On February 21, 1965, Malcolm X addressed a gathering of his followers at the Audubon Ballroom in Washington Heights. As he spoke, three assassins approached the stage and fired sixteen bullets into his body. An hour later, he was dead.

★

opposite MUHAMMAD ALI APPLAUDS VIGOROUSLY AT A NATION OF ISLAM GATHERING. *above* ALI ATTENDS A NATION OF ISLAM MEETING IN A FRUIT OF ISLAM (FOI) UNIFORM.

CHAPTER FOUR

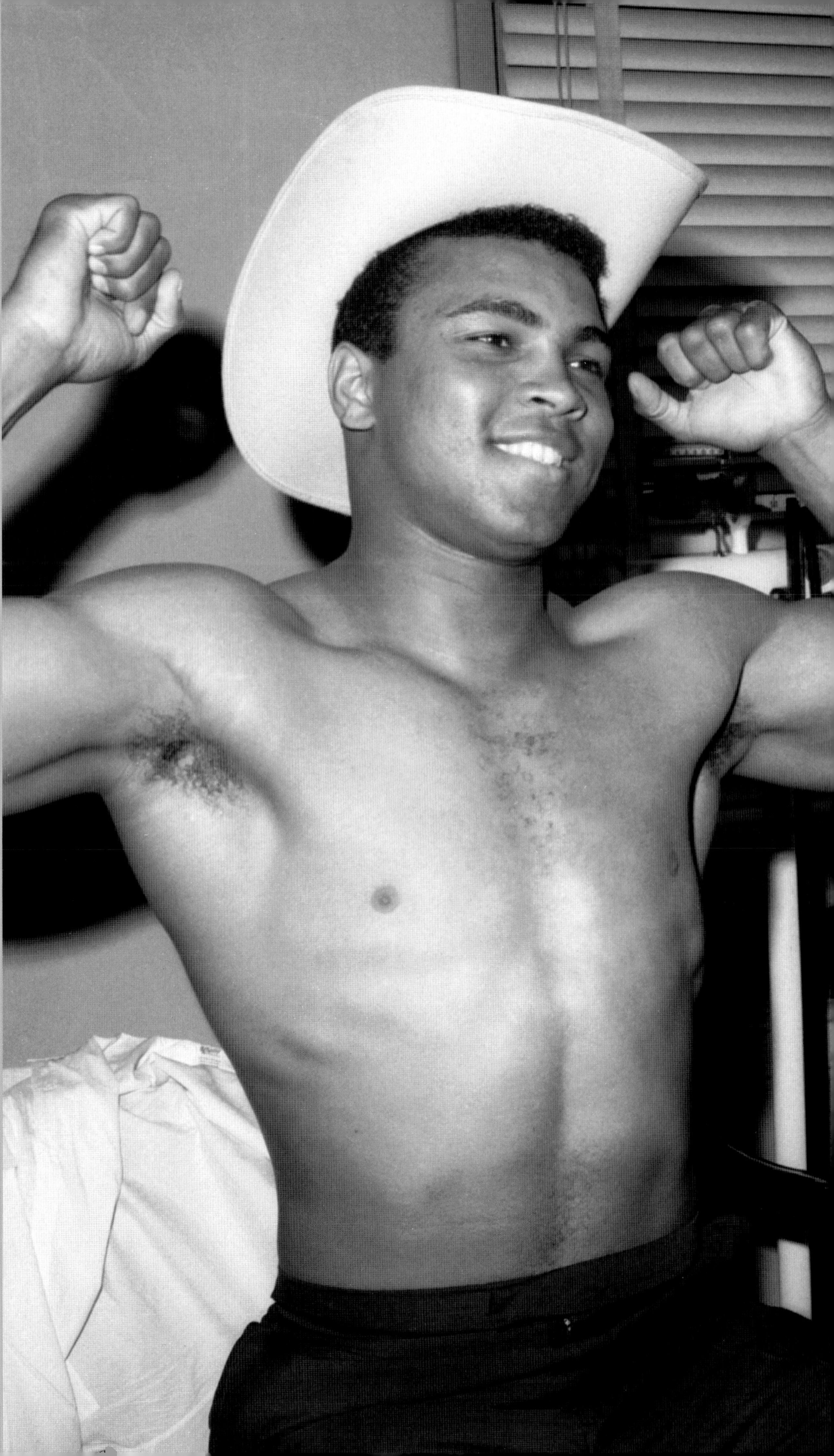

THE MOST BEAUTIFUL FIGHTING MACHINE

"I WANTED HIM TO GET UP, SO I COULD SHOW EVERYONE HOW GREAT I WAS."

— Muhammad Ali, on his reaction to a felled Sonny Liston in their 1965 rematch

There was no way that Muhammad Ali could have imagined the twists and turns his life would take after he joined the Nation of Islam. But one clue came when the first defense of his championship—a May 25, 1965, rematch against Sonny Liston—was relegated to a union hall in Lewiston, Maine.

Jack Dempsey, Joe Louis, and Rocky Marciano had defended the most coveted title in sports in venues like Yankee Stadium and Madison Square Garden. St. Dominic's Arena was akin to a high school gym.

Ali entered the ring to boos; Liston, the possessor of a criminally violent past, to applause.

Two minutes after the fight began, it was over.

opposite AS A "COWBOY," ALI WORE A WHITE HAT.

Ali confronted the bully immediately, rushing across the ring and landing a straight right hand. Liston seemed tentative. A minute into the fight, he threw a jab. Ali leaned back to avoid the blow, pivoted, and retaliated with a right hand counter.

It was a solid punch. There was nothing "phantom" about it, although the speed with which it was thrown left many viewers unable to follow its trajectory.

Liston crumbled awkwardly to the canvas, breaking his fall with his gloves before rolling onto his back. Ali stood over him, demanding that he rise and fight on. Sonny turned onto his chest, bowed his head, and rose to one knee.

Meanwhile, former heavyweight champion Jersey Joe Walcott, the ill-advised choice to referee the fight, had lost control of the action. Ali was dancing around the ring, alternately shouting, jumping, and menacing

Liston. Walcott was unable to restrain him and had no idea what the count was.

Liston rolled onto his back again and stretched his arms behind his head on the canvas. He looked like a man imitating a fighter who had been knocked out. Seventeen seconds after hitting the canvas, he rose. Walcott wiped his gloves and the action resumed.

Ali charged in, throwing punches. Then Walcott heard *Ring Magazine* editor Nat Fleischer shouting, "It's over! He's out!" The referee walked over to Fleischer, leaving the fighters unattended. Finally, he returned, broke the fighters apart, and signaled that the bout was over.

There was no protest from Liston. Whatever his thought processes, two minutes in the ring with Ali seemed to have been enough for him.

ALI VS. FLOYD PATTERSON

Ali's next title defense was against former heavyweight champion Floyd Patterson. But first, there was a confrontation outside the ropes.

Patterson refused to acknowledge Ali by any name other than the one on his birth certificate. He also stated publicly, "The Black Muslim influence must be removed from boxing. I believe the preaching of segregation, hatred, rebellion, and violence is wrong. Cassius Clay is disgracing himself and the Negro race."

Ali responded by calling the challenger "a deaf, dumb, so-called Negro who needs a spanking" and "a white man's slave."

above A RIGHT HAND THAT PRECEDED *THE* RIGHT HAND. ALI MEASURES SONNY LISTON IN THEIR MAY 25, 1965, REMATCH IN LEWISTON, MAINE.

ALI DANCES AROUND A FALLEN SONNY LISTON AS
REFEREE JERSEY JOE WALCOTT SEEKS TO IMPOSE ORDER.

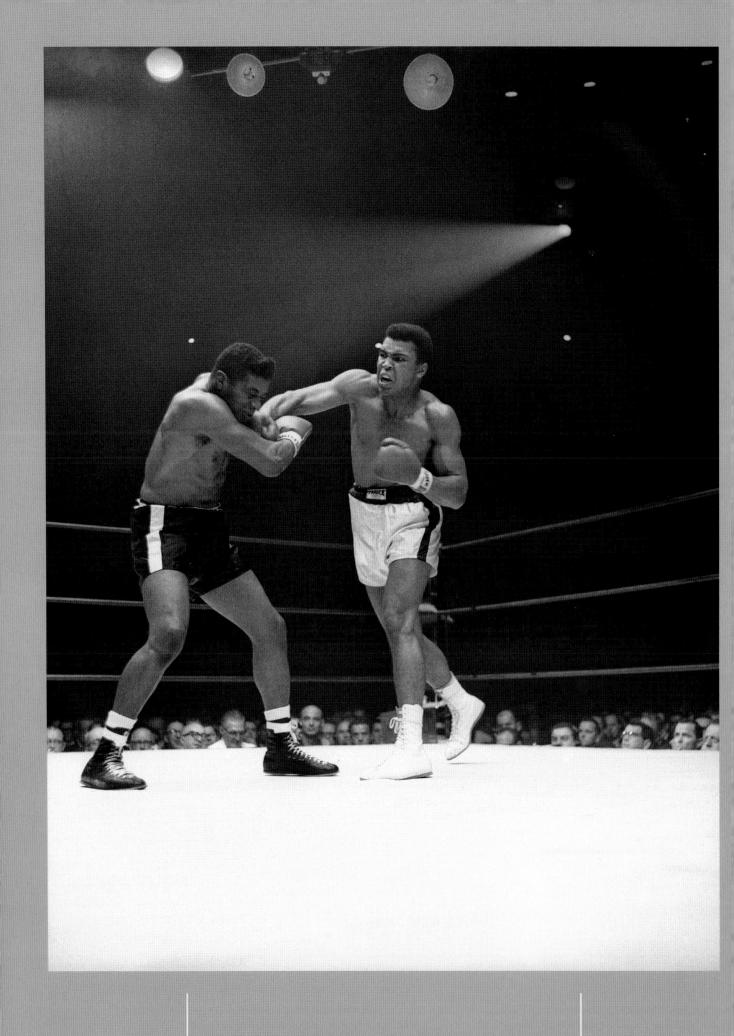

ALI DOMINATED FORMER HEAVYWEIGHT CHAMPION
FLOYD PATTERSON IN LAS VEGAS ON NOVEMBER 22, 1965.

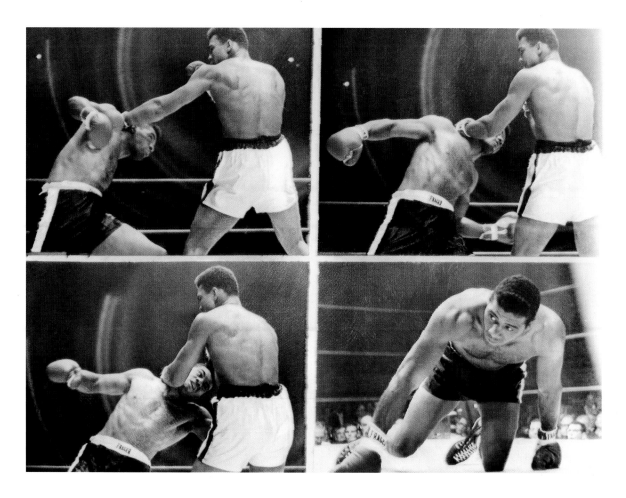

They met in the ring on November 22, 1965, the second anniversary of President Kennedy's assassination. By round six, Patterson was on one knee, a beaten man. He was suffering from excruciating back pain in addition to the other problems caused by Ali's fists. He rose, winced, and proceeded to drag his right foot along the canvas for six more rounds.

There was cruelty in Ali that night that went beyond the normal bounds of prizefighting. Reproached by referee Harold Krause for "chattering" early in the fight, he increased his taunts in direct proportion to Patterson's helplessness. More significantly, he threw hurting blows but never fully committed to imposing a merciful end to Patterson's suffering. He had power over a helpless man in the unsparing confines of a boxing ring and reveled in it. The fight was stopped in the twelfth round.

THE WORLD'S CHAMPION

Ali's next four bouts were contested on foreign soil. He easily defeated George Chuvalo in Canada, Henry Cooper and Brian London in England, and Karl Mildenberger in Germany. He fought abroad in part because his controversial beliefs made him unwelcome and a poor draw at the gate in much of the United States. And he embraced

above ALI FLOORED PATTERSON IN ROUND SIX AND FINISHED HIM OFF IN THE TWELFTH.

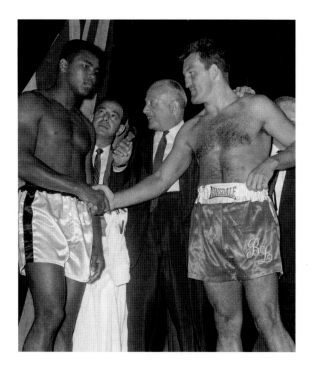

the opportunity to display his skills in other lands.

"Things were beginning to happen electronically," Bob Arum, Ali's promoter at the time, later recalled. "The equipment was getting more sophisticated. We'd never had satellites before. Now, for the first time, we could show a fight live from New York on television in the United Kingdom or vice versa."

The heavyweight championship now truly belonged to the world. But Ali received a lukewarm reception when he returned to the United States. Though his popularity had grown in other nations, he was less of a fan favorite each time he fought at home.

Meanwhile, Ali continued to hone his skills. What he did in prefight buildups was novel for the media. What he did to other heavyweights after the bell sounded was unique in the annals of prizefighting. This wasn't John

Wayne punching out a bad guy in a Hollywood movie. Ali's opponents were flesh and blood warriors with prodigious physical gifts who had spent years learning how to beat down other men. And they were helpless before him.

On November 14, 1966, Ali defended his championship against Cleveland Williams in the Houston Astrodome. Williams was a hard-punching veteran who matched Ali in height, weight, and reach. The two men looked equal at the weigh-in. That perception vanished in the opening seconds of round one.

Ali's hands were blazing fast and his punches packed power. But against Williams, his legs were the most magnificent part of him. He retreated, attacked, then retreated and attacked again, virtually in the same moment. He peppered Williams with jabs followed by straight right hands, moved out of range, then opened fire again.

Williams was an experienced fighter. He'd seen combination punching before. Now, he couldn't see the punches coming. He only felt them.

Ali dominated from the opening bell, knocking the challenger down four times. The carnage was stopped after seven minutes. Over the course of three rounds, Williams had been able to hit the champion a total of three times.

WHAT'S MY NAME?

Ten weeks after devastating Williams, Ali returned to the Astrodome to fight six-foot-six-inch Ernie Terrell,

★

above ALI AND BRIAN LONDON SHAKE HANDS PRIOR TO THEIR 1966 FIGHT IN LONDON.

MUHAMMAD ALI, ARMS RAISED IN VICTORY, TURNS AWAY
FROM AN OUTSTRETCHED CLEVELAND WILLIAMS IN THE
ASTRODOME ON NOVEMBER 14, 1966.

bone, so the injured eye could no longer turn. As the rounds passed, his face was bloody and his spirit broken. Worn and slow, he lumbered about as Ali cruelly berated him, firing sharp, stinging punches and demanding, "What's my name!"

It wasn't a question. It was an executioner's cry. But Ali refused to execute. He preferred to torture. "What's my name! . . . What's my name!"

Unable to do more than endure humiliation and absorb pain, Terrell took a fifteen-round beating. Both the referee and his corner should have stopped it, but no one intervened.

Six weeks later, Ali returned to the ring against Zora Folley at Madison Square Garden. Folley called Ali by his Islamic name. He didn't endeavor to wage war for reasons of national pride, brotherhood, or patriotism. He presented a patient offense and a traditional defense.

His cause was hopeless. Muhammad Ali, at age twenty-five, was the most beautiful fighting machine ever assembled. He knocked Folley out in the seventh round. Afterward, the defeated warrior called his conqueror "the greatest fighter of all time."

"There's no way to train yourself for what he does," Folley elaborated. "The moves, the speed, the punches, the way he changes style every time you think you have him figured. He's smart, the trickiest fighter I've ever seen. He's had twenty-nine fights and acts like he's had a hundred. He could write the book on boxing, and anyone that fights him should be made to read it."

who made the same mistake that Floyd Patterson had made fifteen months earlier. He insisted on referring to Ali as "Clay."

In later years, Ali would be hailed as a man who loved all people and a hero who objected to war as a matter of conscience. But on February 6, 1967, he was still very much in disfavor with the American public. And he exacerbated that situation by torturing Terrell beyond anything that sportsmanship in boxing allows.

As a fight evolves, a fighter weighs the peril that the opponent presents. If that peril drops beneath a certain level, the fighter does one of two things. Most often, he attacks to finish the job. In rare instances, he lays back and, at risk to himself, allows his opponent to finish on his feet with dignity.

Against Terrell, Ali did neither.

Early in the fight, Terrell suffered a fractured bone under his left eye. One of his eye muscles caught on the

opposite (top) ALI IN A CLINCH WITH ERNIE TERRELL. THE CHALLENGER REFUSED TO CALL ALI BY HIS CHOSEN NAME DURING PRE-FIGHT PROMOTION AND SUFFERED FIFTEEN ROUNDS OF TAUNTING AND PUNISHMENT AS A RESULT. *opposite (bottom)* TERRELL (LEFT) AND ALI POSE DURING A PRE-BOUT PROMOTIONAL EVENT. *above* ALI INSPECTS HIS HANDIWORK AFTER SENDING ZORA FOLLEY TO THE CANVAS IN THEIR MARCH 22, 1967, FIGHT AT MADISON SQUARE GARDEN.

CLAY VS. LISTON PROGRAM

A fight program for Ali's rematch against Sonny Liston refused to acknowledge the champion's new name.

ALI VS. LISTON TICKET

The ticket for Ali's first title defense referred to him only as the "champion."

left MUHAMMAD ALI, IN SLIPPERS, READIES FOR A PRE-FIGHT WEIGH-IN. *opposite* WHEN ALI WAS YOUNG, HIS HANDS WERE QUICKER THAN ANY IN THE HISTORY OF THE HEAVYWEIGHT DIVISION.

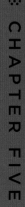

ALI AND VIETNAM

"I AIN'T GOT NO QUARREL WITH THEM VIETCONG."

—Muhammad Ali

Muhammad Ali was not the first black athlete to march to his own drummer and become a flamboyant spectacle. Heavyweight champion Jack Johnson provided that template. But Ali was the first to do so and finish standing, unbroken by an intolerant system. And he set fire to the obstacles that had confined black athletes like Joe Louis and Jackie Robinson.

On April 28, 1967, thirty-seven days after he defeated Zora Folley, Ali arrived at the United States Armed Forces Examining and Entrance Station in Houston. The site was seven-and-a-half miles from the Astrodome, where his fights against Cleveland Williams and Ernie Terrell had been contested.

Ali underwent a physical examination and was led with twenty-five other young men to the ceremony room, where an officer advised them, "You are about to be inducted into the Armed Forces of the United States: in the Army, the Navy, the Air Force, or the Marine Corps, as indicated by the service announced following your name when called. You will take one step forward as your name and service are called, and such step will constitute your induction."

left DEMONSTRATORS GATHER IN HOUSTON TO SUPPORT ALI'S REFUSAL TO ACCEPT INDUCTION INTO THE UNITED STATES ARMED FORCES ON APRIL 28, 1967.

generation took up arms to guard against the Communist threat in Korea. Americans had their say in voting booths. When war came, citizens served when called. Many Americans regarded Ali's talk of individual conscience and personal choice as treason.

Also, Ali had requested exemption from the armed forces on the basis of his belief in the tenets of the Nation of Islam. Thus, his refusal to be inducted acquired an immediate racial component in the eyes of the American public.

Years later, Ali would say of his decision, "I never thought of myself as great when I refused to go into the Army. All I did was stand up for what I believed. Everything I did was according to my conscience. I wasn't trying to be a leader. I just wanted to be free. Freedom means being able to follow your religion, but it also means carrying the responsibility to choose between right and wrong."

But in 1967, different words resonated. Ali was the man who, upon being notified that the Selective Service System had declared him eligible for the military draft, famously proclaimed, "I ain't got no quarrel with them Vietcong."

When "Cassius Marcellus Clay" was called, Ali stood motionless. He was advised that the refusal to accept a lawful induction order constituted a felony, and responded that he was aware of the consequences. Later that day, he issued a statement to the media that read, in part, "I have searched my conscience and find I cannot be true to my belief in my religion by accepting such a call. My decision is a private and individual one. In taking it, I am dependent solely upon Allah as the final judge of these actions brought about by my own conscience."

Seen through the lens of history, Ali's decision to refuse induction is more understandable and far more accepted today than it was at the time. An entire generation of Americans had fought a "good war" in Europe and the Far East to preserve democracy. Then another

A PRICE TO PAY

Boxing passed judgment on Ali before the federal government could. Within an hour of his refusal to step forward in Houston, the New York State Athletic Commission suspended his boxing license and withdrew its recognition of him as heavyweight champion.

★

above THE COLLAR TIGHTENS. ALI IN THE LOBBY OF THE FEDERAL COURT BUILDING IN HOUSTON ON JUNE 19, 1967, THE FIRST DAY OF HIS CRIMINAL TRIAL ON CHARGES OF REFUSING INDUCTION INTO THE UNITED STATES ARMED FORCES.

DESPITE HIS EXILE FROM BOXING, ALI'S VOICE WAS
NOT SILENCED.

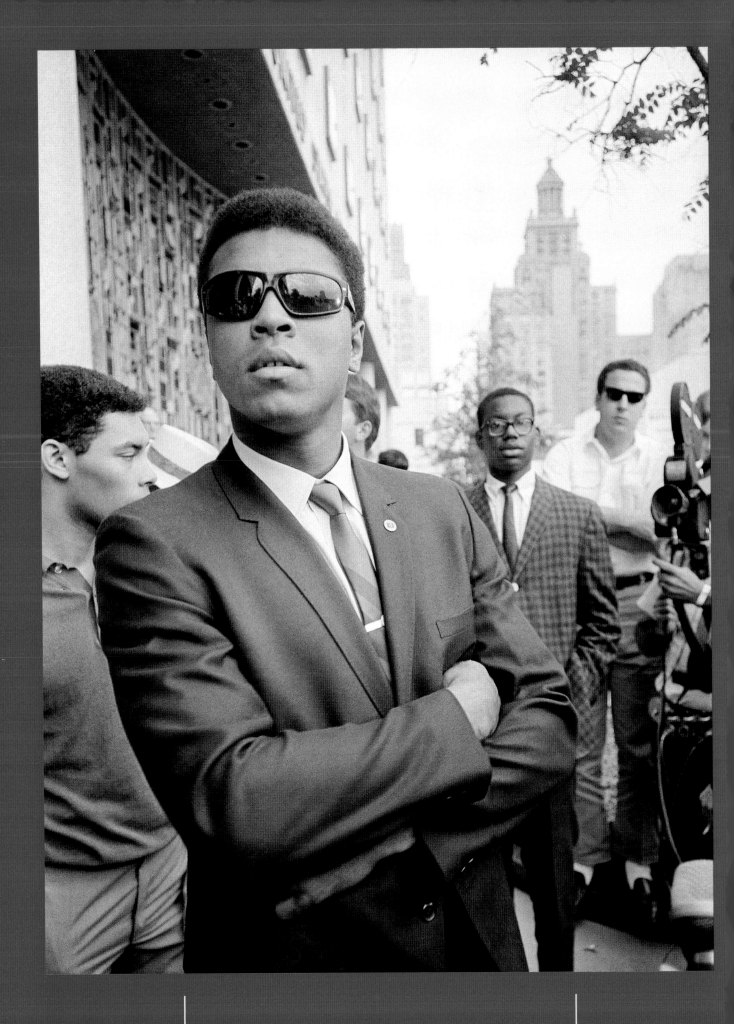

ALTHOUGH ALI WAS NOW INACTIVE AS A FIGHTER,
IT SEEMED AS THOUGH THERE WERE CAMERAS
WHEREVER HE WENT.

"Due process of law hadn't even begun," television commentator Howard Cosell later noted. "Yet they took away his livelihood because he failed the test of political and social conformity, and it took him seven years to get his title back."

Ten days after refusing induction, Ali was indicted by a grand jury in Houston. On June 19, 1967, his criminal trial began. The following afternoon, the case went to a jury of his "peers." They deliberated for twenty minutes before returning a verdict of guilty.

Ali asked the court to sentence him at once. Judge Joe Ingraham then imposed a sentence of five years' imprisonment and a ten-thousand-dollar fine: or, the maximum penalty allowable under law.

An appeal was filed in federal circuit court. That would keep Ali out of jail for the time being. But it couldn't get him back into a boxing ring.

Judge Ingraham instructed that Ali's passport be confiscated. Combined with the loss of his license to box in the United States, that left the heavyweight champion of the world unable to ply his trade in what would have been the prime years of his career.

ALI IN EXILE

Without a résumé to attract corporate employers, Ali toured the country doing the one thing that came more naturally to him than fighting—talking. He undertook a series of speaking engagements on university campuses.

The sixties were in full bloom. America's colleges were incubators for youthful rebellion. Still, Ali's speeches received mixed reviews. Students who adored him for refusing to go to war were appalled when he reiterated Islam's teachings that women should be submissive to their husbands and leave the governance of society to men.

★

above AS THE 1960S PROGRESSED, ALI FOUND HIMSELF AT THE VORTEX OF THE ANTI-WAR MOVEMENT.

They were less than enamored when he complained about the odor of marijuana that sometimes drifted through the air. Applause for his message of black pride was offset by antagonism toward his separatist racial views.

Yet through it all, Ali's voice was heard.

Senator Ted Kennedy later observed, "Muhammad's actions contributed enormously to the debate about whether the United States should be in Vietnam and galvanized some of his admirers to join protests against the war for the first time."

Arthur Ashe said of Ali, "This man helped give an entire people a belief in themselves and the will to make themselves better. But Ali didn't just change the image that African-Americans have of themselves. He opened the eyes of a lot of white people to the potential of African-Americans: who we are and what we can be."

Then the wheel of fortune turned again. There was no state athletic commission in Georgia. Local municipalities could do pretty much what they wanted insofar as boxing was concerned. In mid-1970, a powerful black state legislator in Georgia named Leroy Johnson leaned heavily on Atlanta mayor Sam Massell and called in his political IOUs. After much back and forth, Massell relented and gave Johnson what he wanted.

In the heart of what had once been the Confederate States of America, forty months after he was exiled from the ring, with a criminal conviction still hanging over his head, Muhammad Ali was allowed to return to boxing.

★

above ALI SPOKE OFTEN ON COLLEGE CAMPUSES DURING HIS YEARS IN EXILE.

ALI HELPS AN ANTI-WAR PROTESTOR IMPROVE THE
VISIBILITY OF HIS SIGN.

CLAY, AKA ALI, VS. UNITED STATES DECISION

A unanimous opinion by the United States Court vindicated Ali in the eyes of the law.

ALI VS. USA FILM POSTER

The 1970 documentary *a/k/a Cassius Clay* broke new ground in the public perception of Ali.

left ALI ON HIS WAY TO SEE JAMES EARL JONES STAR ON BROADWAY IN *THE GREAT WHITE HOPE*. *opposite* ALI WAVES TO HIS FANS AS HE ENTERS THE ARMY INDUCTION CENTER IN HOUSTON, TEXAS.

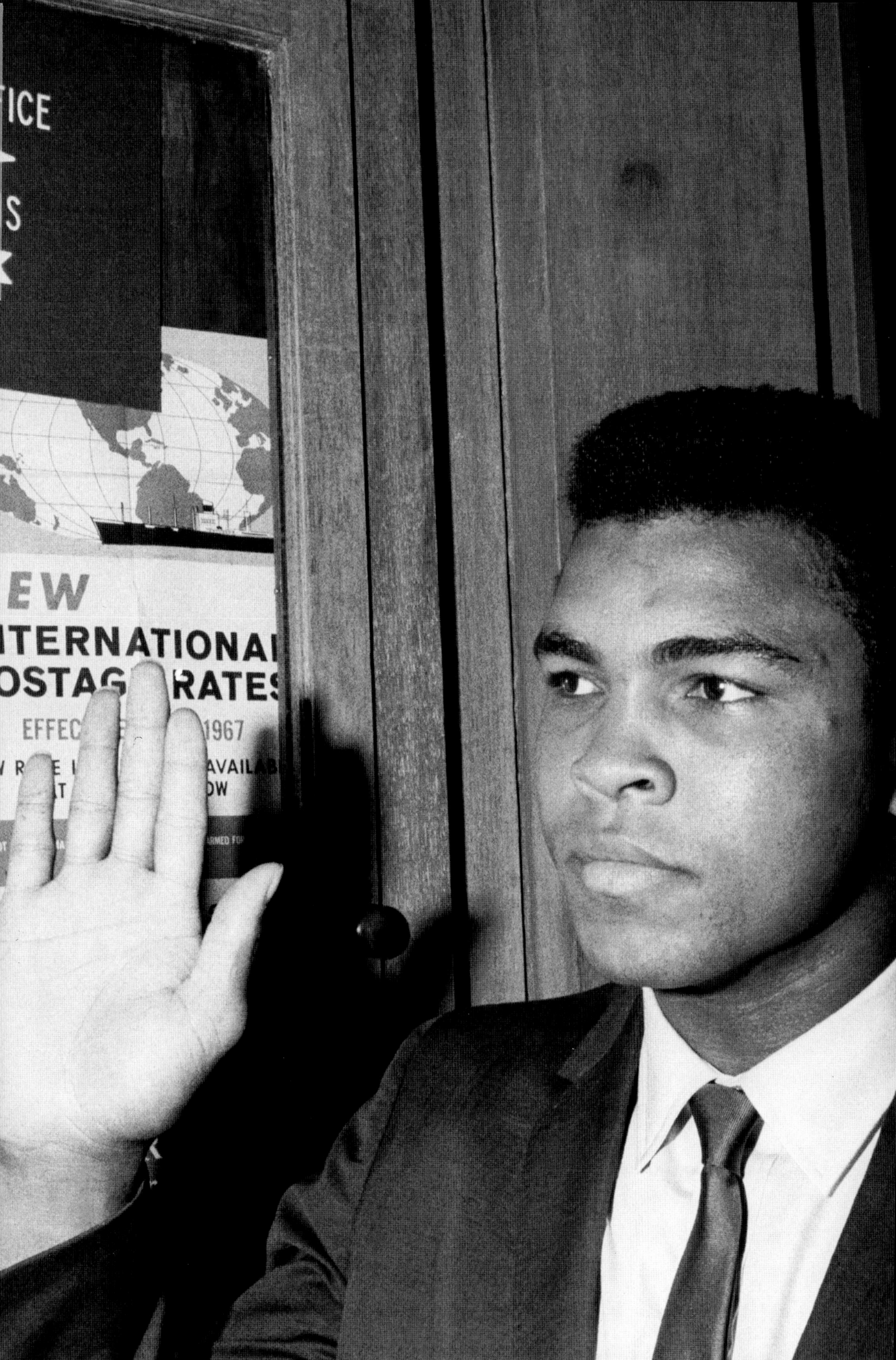
FICE
EW
NTERNATIONAL
OSTAG RATES
EFFEC 1967
AVAILAB
OW

CHAPTER SIX

THE FIGHT
OF THE
CENTURY

"ON THAT NIGHT, THEY'LL BE WAITING EVERYWHERE. ENG-
LAND, FRANCE, ITALY. EGYPT AND ISRAEL WILL DECLARE
A FORTY-FIVE-MINUTE TRUCE. SAUDI ARABIA, IRAQ, IRAN;
EVEN RED CHINA AND FORMOSA. NOT SINCE TIME BEGAN
HAS THERE BEEN A NIGHT LIKE THIS."

— Muhammad Ali, on his upcoming "Fight of the Century" against Joe Frazier

On October 26, 1970, Muhammad Ali returned from exile to fight "Irish" Jerry Quarry in Atlanta.

Ali had been driven from boxing at a time when his popularity was dwindling. He returned to the sport in a city with a large black population as a hero who'd confronted an unjust system and remained unbowed. Boxing has never been bashful about exploiting ethnic rivalries. The promotion of Ali versus Quarry was no exception. But in the end, the confines of a boxing ring are apolitical. Quarry's subsequent words about fighting Ali put the matter in perspective.

"I wasn't fighting for any race, creed, or color that night," Quarry said. "I was fight-ing for money. The crowd was 90 percent black and all for Ali, but that didn't motivate

opposite ALI, IN HIS PRIME, STRIKES A CLASSIC POSE.

me or intimidate me either. When I got in the ring, it was just another fight, even though the opponent was Ali. I wasn't fighting against a symbol. I was fighting a fighter, who had two arms and two legs just like me."

Ali's arms and legs were slower than they'd been before. He was more than three years older, a few pounds heavier, and a bit less muscled than he'd been for his last fight. He was still faster and more fluid than any heavyweight alive. But he no longer moved like the young Ali.

Round one of Ali-Quarry began with Muhammad on his toes, circling to his left as he'd done in past fights. But the seeming effortlessness of motion that had characterized Cassius Clay and the young Ali was no longer there. There was a new consciousness to his movement. And he was hittable.

But Quarry's skin betrayed him before he could test Ali. Not the color of his skin; its toughness. In round three, a sharp right hand opened a gaping wound above his right eye. The bone was visible. Referee Tony Perez had no choice but to stop the fight.

Then, thanks to the intervention of the federal courts, the Ali road show moved north. With the appeal of his criminal conviction still pending, Ali applied for a court order that would allow him to fight in New York. United States District Judge Walter Mansfield ruled that the New York State Athletic Commission's denial of a boxing license to Ali violated the "equal protection" clause of the Fourteenth Amendment to the Constitution of the United States. The commission, Mansfield noted, regularly granted licenses to accused and convicted felons.

above ALI AND JERRY QUARRY STARE AT ONE ANOTHER ACROSS THE MEDICAL EXAMINER'S TABLE ON THE MORNING OF THEIR FIGHT. *opposite* ACCOMPANIED BY CORNERMAN BUNDINI BROWN, ALI TAKES A VICTORY LAP AROUND THE RING AFTER STOPPING QUARRY IN HIS OCTOBER 26, 1970, RETURN TO BOXING.

AN EXHAUSTED ALI READIES FOR ONE MORE ROUND
AGAINST OSCAR BONAVENA AS TRAINER ANGELO
DUNDEE GIVES INSTRUCTIONS.

That set the stage for Ali to fight Argentina's Oscar Bonavena at Madison Square Garden on December 7, 1970. It was not lost on veterans groups that the fight would take place on the twenty-ninth anniversary of the Japanese attack on Pearl Harbor.

Bonavena was everything that Mark Twain warned about when he wrote, "The best swordsman in the world doesn't need to fear the second-best swordsman in the world. No; the person for him to be afraid of is some ignorant antagonist who has never had a sword in his hand before. He does the thing he ought not to do; and often it catches the expert out and ends him on the spot."

Metaphorically speaking, Bonavena had previously held a sword. But he was oblivious to sword-fighting etiquette. He whacked Ali on the protective cup twice in the opening round and brawled from start to finish.

It was an ugly fight. The end came in the fifteenth round, when Ali pulled a left hook—a punch he rarely threw with authority—out of his bag of tricks. Bonavena went down as though hit with a baseball bat, rose, and was knocked down twice more. The final knockdown ended the fight.

Then Ali confronted the man who would become his greatest rival: Joe Frazier.

"SMOKIN' JOE"

Frazier had grown up poor in rural South Carolina. He quit school in ninth grade, married at age sixteen, and took a job in a slaughterhouse to support his family. He began boxing in 1962, and won a gold medal in the heavyweight division at the Tokyo Olympics two years later.

above JOE FRAZIER AND ALI TRADE WORDS BEFORE THEIR HISTORIC FIRST FIGHT WITH MADISON SQUARE GARDEN PUBLICIST JOHN CONDON BETWEEN THEM.

Frazier went by the nickname "Smokin' Joe." No one likened him to a ballet dancer or butterfly. In the ring, he went straight at every opponent and reduced his fights to wars of attrition. His defense was better than many people understood. In some respects, his head movement was superior to Ali's. But the heart of his game was relentless aggression, volume punching, a devastating left hook, and the wisdom to not confuse himself by employing an alternate plan of attack.

Ali mocked Frazier's constant aggression as the work of an untutored, perhaps uneducable, fighter. They would share a boxing ring for forty-one rounds over the course of three fights that spanned three-and-a-half years. When their wars were over, it was clear that Joe's style was ideally suited to his own physical skills and temperament. More important, it was the perfect style with which to do battle against Ali.

During Ali's years in exile, Frazier had fought his way to the heavyweight title. But he knew that he'd never be accepted as a true champion unless and until he beat Ali. The moment of truth came at Madison Square Garden on March 8, 1971, in a battle known as the Fight of the Century.

The prefight promotion captured the attention of the world. For the first time in history, two undefeated fighters, each with a legitimate claim to the heavyweight championship, would be fighting for the throne. The story line was captivating. And at times, it was ugly.

Ali had the habit of saying anything that crossed

his mind to build his own confidence and crush an opponent's ego. As Frazier talked clumsily at prefight press conferences, Muhammad would use his silver tongue to slash Joe to pieces metaphorically. Worse, in playing the role of an antiestablishment hero, Ali labeled Frazier an Uncle Tom.

Dave Wolf, a former sports editor for *Life* magazine who was in the Frazier camp, later recalled, "What Ali did was turn Joe into a black white hope. He isolated Joe from the black community. He constantly equated Joe with the white power structure and said things like, 'Any black person who's for Joe Frazier is a traitor.' It was cruel;

★

above ALI PREPARES TO RECLAIM HIS CROWN. *opposite* THROUGHOUT HIS EXILE AND RETURN TO BOXING, ALI MAINTAINED THAT HE'D BEEN UNFAIRLY STRIPPED OF HIS TITLE AND WAS THE TRUE HEAVYWEIGHT CHAMPION OF THE WORLD.

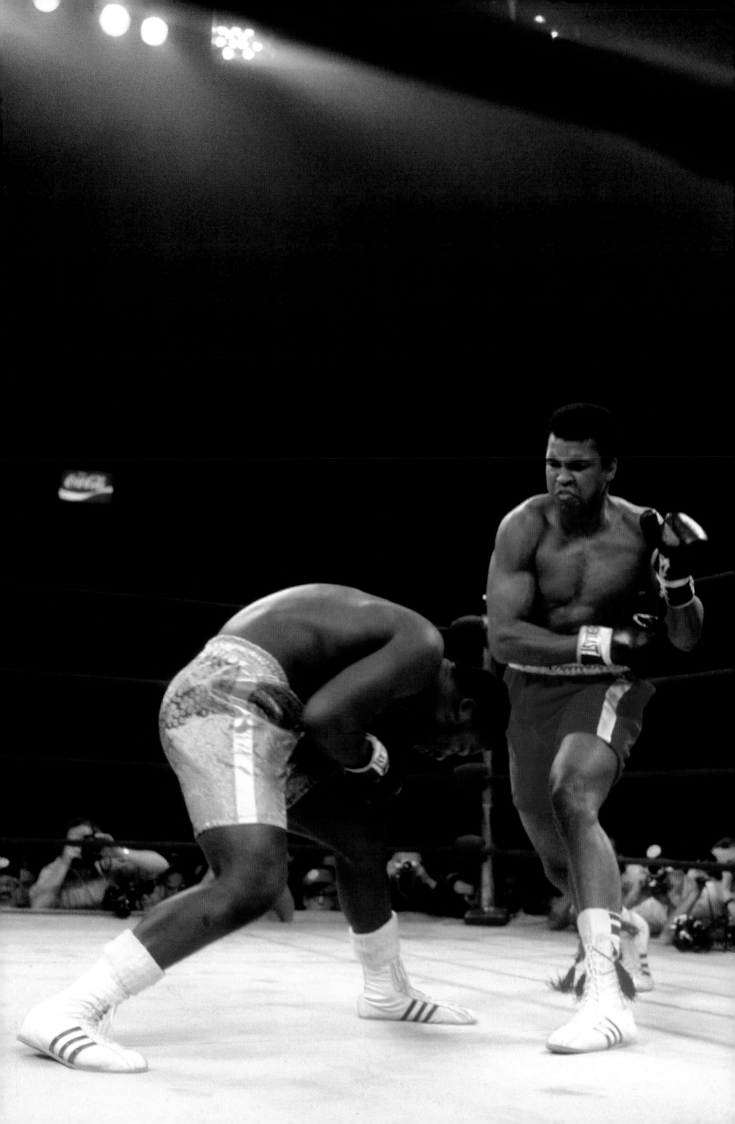

that's all. Joe, as a result of his background and upbringing, was almost the stereotypic black person Ali claimed to be fighting for. Yet Ali demeaned Joe at every turn."

But of all the derogatory things that Ali said about Frazier during the buildup to the Fight of the Century, none was more erroneous than this: "You take a man like Frazier, a good fighter, but a simple, hard-working fellow; he's not built for this kind of pressure, the eyes of that many people upon him."

In truth, Frazier fought with a singlemindedness of purpose that was resistant to psychological pressure. Against Ali, he would attack, fight through whatever blows came his way, and keep attacking. He would aim for Muhammad's body, not his head, because the body was less elusive. He would demean Ali with his fists the way Ali had demeaned him with his mouth. And he wouldn't call his opponent "Ali."

"I've proved I can take a punch," Frazier said before the fight. "But what about Clay? Will he come apart when I put something on him; when I start smoking where he lives? He can keep that pretty head; I don't want it. What I'm going to do is try to pull them kidneys out."

THE FIGHT

When the historic night arrived, Ali wore red satin trunks and a matching robe, each with white trim. Frazier sported green brocade with gold woven in. Referee Arthur Mercante gave the fighters final instructions in the center of the ring. Ali jawed at his opponent. Frazier nodded and smiled. The fighters returned to their corners. Ali held his hands out toward Mecca, palms open, and said a brief prayer—as he'd done before each fight since publicly

opposite JOE FRAZIER DUCKS UNDER A MUHAMMAD ALI RIGHT HAND IN THEIR MARCH 8, 1971, FIGHT OF THE CENTURY. *above* EARLY ON, ALI WAS STILL QUICK ENOUGH TO ELUDE FRAZIER'S CONCUSSIVE LEFT HOOKS.

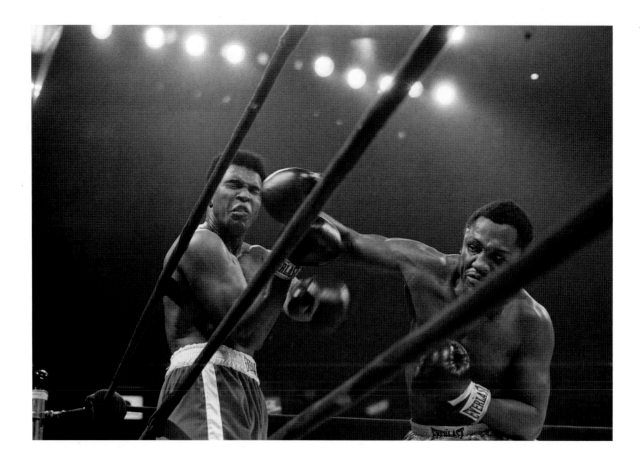

acknowledging his conversion to the Nation of Islam. Frazier received final words of encouragement from his trainer, Yank Durham. The bell rang. The "Fight of the Century" had begun.

In the past, Ali had gone to great lengths in the ring to avoid being hit. Against Frazier, he danced for the first minute. Then he came down off his toes and started punching. Conventional wisdom is that the change in style came about because his legs were no longer what they'd once been. It's also possible that Ali stopped floating to his left on tiptoes because Frazier's head seemed so accessible to Muhammad's fists. Frazier moved to his own beat; not in reaction to his opponent's offense. Once Ali understood the pattern, he settled down and punched.

But nothing about Frazier was fragile. Though Ali would demonstrate as good a chin as Joe, he would learn that he wasn't the only man in the ring with an indomitable will that night.

Ali mounted a sustained assault in round nine; the one time in the fight when Frazier took a backward step. Apart from that, it was Joe who landed the harder blows. Ali was hit with more crushing punches than he'd been hit with during the entirety of his earlier championship reign. Each time his head snapped to the left, courtesy of a Frazier left hook, he shook his head as if to say to the crowd, "That didn't hurt."

above AS ALI-FRAZIER I WORE ON, FRAZIER FOUND A HOME FOR HIS OWN RIGHT HAND.

JOE FRAZIER MOVES TO A NEUTRAL CORNER AFTER
LANDING A LEFT HOOK THAT HE AND ALI WOULD
REMEMBER THROUGHOUT THEIR LIVES.

But the punches did hurt. And over time, they took a heavy toll.

In round eleven, Ali was all but out on his feet. He survived through trickery. Dropping his hands, he shimmied backward toward his corner, convincing Frazier that he was playing possum.

As the fifteenth and final round began, Frazier was leading narrowly on two scorecards and comfortably ahead on the third. Ali was more tired and beaten up than he'd ever been. His hands low, he began to throw a right hand that wouldn't have done much damage had it landed. Frazier got off first, launching a monstrous left hook that landed flush on Ali's jaw and put him down.

Only a handful of men who ever fought could have taken the punishment that Ali endured that night and risen from Frazier's blow. Ali was on his feet at the count of four. Two minutes and thirty seconds remained in the fight. He survived till the final bell.

Frazier was awarded a unanimous decision.

The cover of the next issue of *Sports Illustrated* pictured Ali falling to the canvas. A banner superimposed across the top of the image read, "End of the Ali Legend."

How wrong they were.

★

opposite THE MORNING AFTER LOSING THE "FIGHT OF THE CENTURY," ALI FACED THE MEDIA AGAIN. *above* SOON, MUHAMMAD WAS BACK IN THE GYM, MAKING PLANS TO REGAIN THE HEAVYWEIGHT CROWN.

ALI VS. FRAZIER PENNANT

Ali-Frazier I gave rise to all kinds of merchandising and memorabilia.

ALI VS. FRAZIER POSTER

A promotional poster for the only Harlem closed-circuit showing of Ali-Frazier I.

left ALI AFTER A WORKOUT IN MIAMI'S FIFTH STREET GYM PRIOR TO HIS FIRST FIGHT AGAINST JOE FRAZIER. *opposite* ALI'S SELF-IMAGE WAS TESTED BY HIS FIRST CAREER DEFEAT. ULTIMATELY, HE WOULD EMERGE STRONGER BECAUSE OF IT

CHAPTER SEVEN

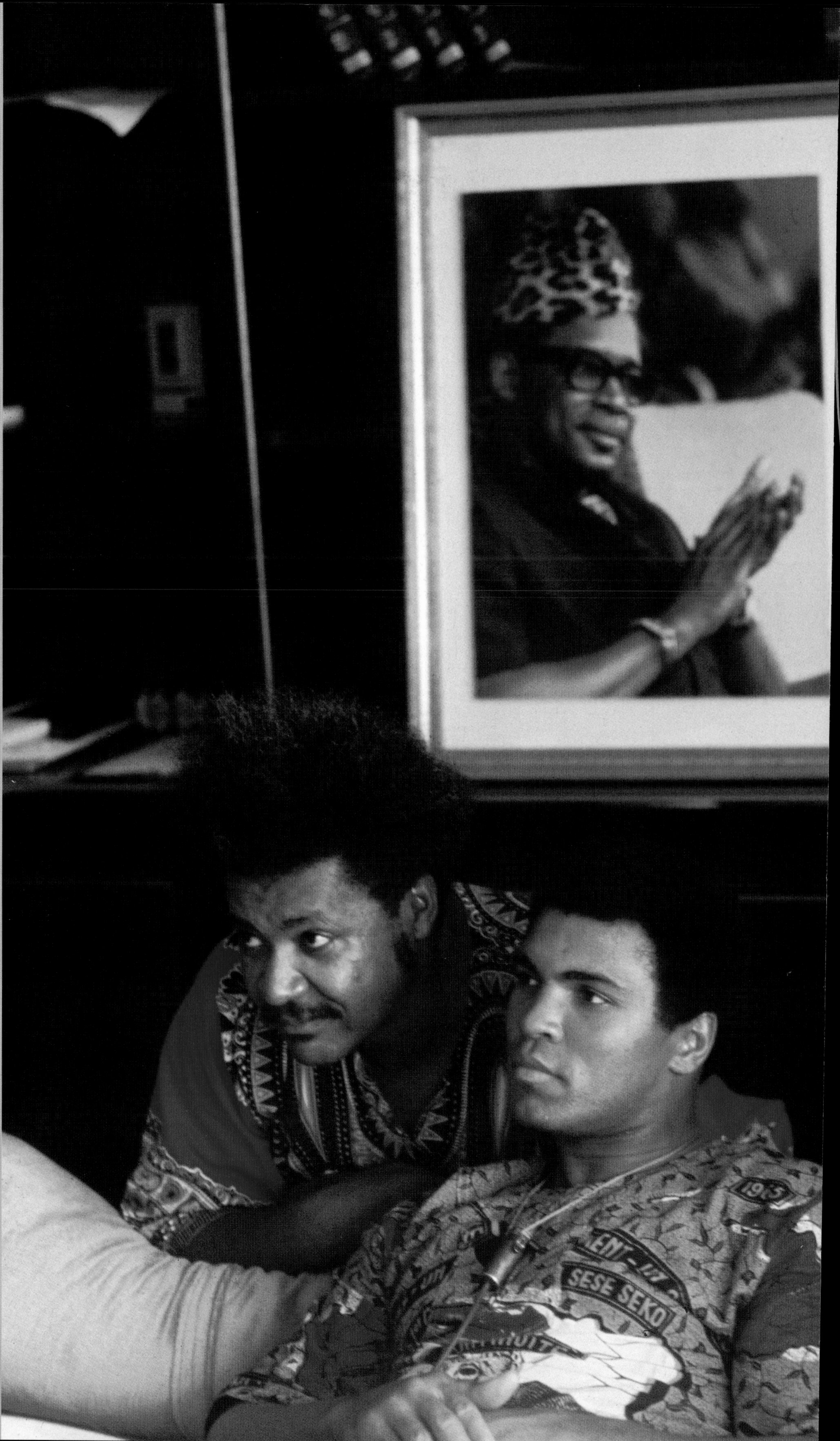

THE RUMBLE IN THE JUNGLE

"GEORGE HITS HARD. I KNOW THAT. BUT HITTING POWER DON'T MEAN NOTHING IF YOU CAN'T FIND NOTHING TO HIT."
—Muhammad Ali

Muhammad Ali's fans were disconsolate after his loss to Joe Frazier. In their minds, the fight had been a confrontation between the forces of good and an unjust social order, and the bad guys had prevailed.

But Ali's head remained high. One day after the "Fight of the Century," hours after hospital x-rays of his grotesquely swollen jaw revealed no fracture, Muhammad met with reporters.

"Just lost a fight, that's all," he said. "There are more important things to worry about in life. Probably be a better man for it."

Each fighter had profoundly harmed the other. Referee Arthur Mercante later recalled, "Both of their faces were misshapen afterward. Ali's face was no longer round. Frazier's was all bruised, swollen, and cut up. In a way, it was horrible watching their features change. But it was history in the making, an incredible fight."

opposite UNDER THE WATCHFUL EYES OF ZAIRE'S PRESIDENT, MOBUTU SESE SEKO, DON KING AND ALI AWAITED THE RUMBLE IN THE JUNGLE.

On June 28, 1971, sixteen weeks after losing to Frazier, Ali received some good news. The United States Supreme Court, citing technical errors in the handling of his case, reversed his conviction for refusing induction into the United States Army.

Thereafter, the rehabilitation of Ali's ring career began. On July 26th, he knocked out Jimmy Ellis, who had the distinction of being both a former Ali sparring partner and a claimant to the heavyweight title during Muhammad's exile from boxing. Victories over Buster Mathis, Jurgen Blin, and Mac Foster followed. Next, Ali defeated three previously vanquished foes—George Chuvalo, Jerry Quarry, and Floyd Patterson—mixed in with victories over Al "Blue" Lewis, Bob Foster, and Joe Bugner.

THE EMERGENCE OF GEORGE FOREMAN

Following his battle against Ali, Joe Frazier was hospitalized for several weeks. Much of that stay was occasioned by treatment for high blood pressure, a preexisting condition. But the forty-five minutes he'd spent trading blows with Ali were also a factor. Frazier didn't fight again in 1971 and entered the ring only twice in 1972, both times against mediocre opposition. In early 1973, Smokin' Joe journeyed to Jamaica to defend his title against George Foreman.

Foreman had won a gold medal in the heavyweight division at the 1968 Mexico City Olympics. He was twenty-five years old, undefeated as a professional, and

above ALI VANQUISHED, THEN CONSOLED, A BEATEN BUSTER MATHIS.

AFTER LOSING TO JOE FRAZIER, ALI TOOK TO THE ROAD
ONCE MORE.

ALI TURNS A CHILDLIKE STROLL INTO AN OCCASION
FOR ROADWORK.

had knocked out thirty-four of the thirty-seven men he'd faced. But none of his opponents had been world-class fighters. Frazier figured him for a soft touch.

Foreman annihilated Frazier, knocking him down six times in less than six minutes of fighting. Referee Arthur Mercante, the man who'd raised Joe's hand in victory after his fight against Ali, stopped the bout in the second round.

George Foreman was now heavyweight champion of the world.

ALI'S COMEBACK DERAILED

Two months after Frazier's defeat, Ali fought an unknown heavyweight named Ken Norton in San Diego.

Norton had learned to box during a four-year stint in the United States Marines. More significantly, he'd been a sparring partner for Joe Frazier and was trained by Eddie Futch, who assisted Yank Durham in training Joe for the first Ali-Frazier fight and would take over the reins in August 1973 when Durham died.

Against Norton in round two, Ali pulled away from a jab and backed into the ropes. Norton followed with another jab and a straight right hand. The punch broke Ali's jaw. He could move his jawbone with his tongue. He refused to quit and fought the rest of the fight in excruciating pain. Norton was awarded a split decision.

"He's an incredibly gritty son of a bitch," Dr. Ferdie Pacheco, one of Ali's cornermen, said years later. "The pain must have been awful. He couldn't fight his fight

because he had to protect his jaw. And still, he fought the whole twelve rounds. Underneath all that beauty, there was an ugly Teamsters Union trucker at work."

The toughness that Ali showed against Ken Norton gave fans yet another reason to like him. All the suspicions that had been voiced about his courage when he was "an unhittable pretty boy who danced" were discarded.

At the same time, cultural vindication was on the horizon. The American people were turning against the war in Vietnam. And whatever they thought of Ali's beliefs, there was widespread recognition that he was a man of principle who had sacrificed enormously for what he believed in.

Ali resisted efforts to brand his refusal to be inducted

★

above ON DECEMBER 26, 1971, ALI KNOCKED BLIN OUT IN THE SEVENTH ROUND.

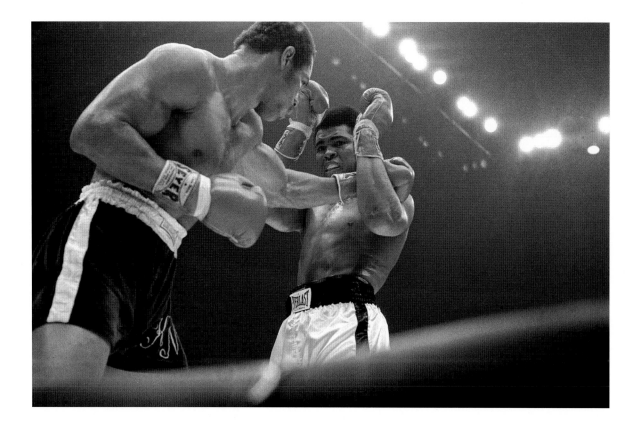

into the armed forces as heroic. But his legacy of principled disobedience was now in place. Many people were beginning to feel that he'd been wronged. And they felt badly that the good part of his career as a fighter appeared to be over.

"Promoters deal in names," Jimmy Cannon wrote. "Ali has a big name and not much to defend it with. He is the guy the hungry kids want to get their hands on. He is a loser now, and they match old losers with young winners."

ALI-FRAZIER II

On September 10, 1973, six months after his jaw was broken, Ali won a close but unanimous decision in a rematch against Ken Norton. That cleared the way for a January 28, 1974, rematch against Joe Frazier at Madison Square Garden.

Those who consider Muhammad Ali vs. Joe Frazier to be the greatest trilogy in boxing history don't dwell on their second fight. It was well short of spectacular. Indeed, the prefight action outside the ring might have been more compelling than the action in it.

Five days before Ali-Frazier II, the combatants met with Howard Cosell in an ABC television studio to discuss their first fight. Frazier mentioned Ali's visit to the hospital after their initial encounter. Ali's pride wouldn't abide the comment. He answered Frazier, saying, "I wasn't gonna talk about the hospital. Everybody knows

---

★

above ON MARCH 31, 1973, ALI SUFFERED HIS SECOND PROFESSIONAL LOSS AT THE HANDS OF UNHERALDED KEN NORTON.

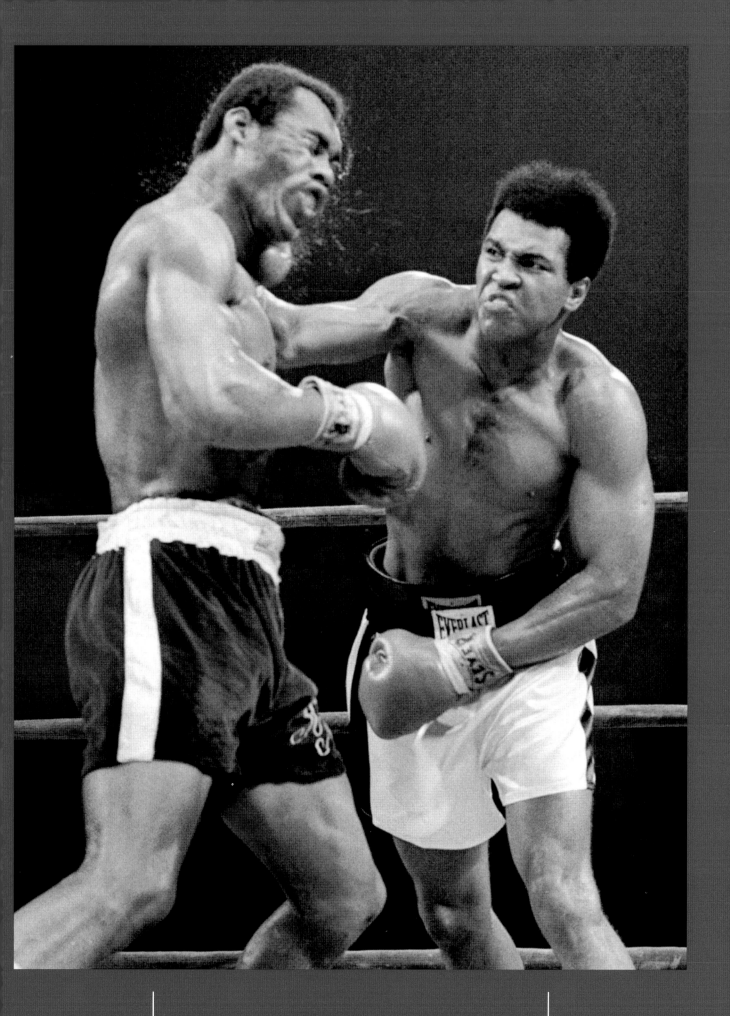

DESPITE SUFFERING A BROKEN JAW IN ROUND TWO, ALI FOUGHT IN THE TRENCHES WITH NORTON FOR TEN MORE ROUNDS. AFTER THIS FIGHT, MUHAMMAD'S TOUGHNESS WAS QUESTIONED NO MORE.

I went to the hospital for ten minutes. You were in the hospital for three weeks. You're ignorant, Joe."

"Ignorant" was the trigger. Frazier's lack of education was a sore spot for Joe. He rose from his seat, stood over Ali, and demanded, "Why'd you call me ignorant?" Ali's brother, Rahaman, was in the studio. He climbed onto the stage and walked toward Frazier, who turned and snapped, "You want to get in this too?"

At that point, Ali stood up and grabbed Frazier in a bear hug. Ali was playing. Frazier wasn't. He threw Ali to the floor. Both entourages converged as the two fighters rolled on the stage. Finally, they were separated.

Later that day, as he drove back to training camp, Frazier chortled, "Did you see how wide his eyes opened up? Now I really got him scared."

If Ali was scared of anything on January 28, it was fatigue. Dancing even less than he had in their first fight, he clinched whenever Frazier got inside, stalling Joe's momentum and defusing the big left hooks that Frazier had landed in their first encounter. The fight was

opposite ALI READIED FOR HIS SECOND FIGHT AGAINST JOE FRAZIER WITH A PROMISE OF THINGS TO COME *above* MUHAMMAD OUTPOINTED JOE IN THEIR JANUARY 28, 1974, CONFRONTATION. BUT BY THEN, FRAZIER HAD LOST THE TITLE TO GEORGE FOREMAN.

scheduled for twelve rounds. Frazier never got on track. Ali potshotted him with jabs and right hands throughout the night en route to a unanimous-decision triumph.

ALI-FOREMAN BECOMES A REALITY

Two months after Ali defeated Joe Frazier, George Foreman defended his title with a devastating second-round knockout of Ken Norton.

Ali had fought fifty-one rounds against Frazier and Norton: winning twice, losing twice, and failing to knock either man down. Foreman had knocked each man out in less than two rounds, sending them to the canvas a total of nine times.

Foreman, at that point in his life, was a menacing, brooding presence. Asked if he liked to talk to his opponent during a fight, as Ali did, George answered, "I never get a chance to talk much in the ring. By the time I begin to know a fellow, it's over."

Within the boxing community, Foreman was regarded as an irresistible, indestructible force. He was as unbeatable as—say—Sonny Liston.

It was inevitable that Ali would challenge Foreman for the heavyweight championship. Once the contracts were signed, Muhammad heard whispers that he'd never heard before. Not only was he a heavy underdog; there were fears for his well-being.

above ALI WAS GREETED BY CHEERING FANS THROUGHOUT HIS STAY IN ZAIRE.

IN THE PRE-FIGHT FESTIVITIES, MUHAMMAD NICKNAMED
GEORGE FOREMAN THE "MUMMY" AND PROMISED TO
DANCE CIRCLES AROUND HIM.

GEORGE FOREMAN, MUHAMMAD ALI, AND "THE ROPE-A-DOPE."

Ali-Foreman was scheduled for September 25, 1974, in Zaire, the domain of dictator Mobutu Sese Seko. Mobuto wanted to make his nation a destination for world travelers and, more important, raise his own profile. He agreed on behalf of his country to part with the then-extraordinary sum of ten million dollars to finance the fight.

Ali dubbed the impending encounter "The Rumble in the Jungle." Don King, who was on a world stage for the first time as a front man for the two corporations behind the fight—Hemdale Film and Video Techniques—embellished that theme. Throughout the promotion, King waxed eloquent about the glories of a fight between two men of African ancestry in the heart of Africa for the heavyweight championship of the world.

"I was good," King said years later. "Ali made me great."

In Zaire, Ali picked up enough dialect to say "kill him" in the local vernacular. He then introduced a slogan for the people of Zaire to chant wherever he went: "Ali bomaye!" ("Ali, kill him!") Soon, those words had taken root in the African soil. Ali needed to do nothing more than pump his fist in the air to hear "Ali bomaye! Ali bomaye!"

Eight days before Ali-Foreman was scheduled to take place, Foreman suffered a deep gash above his right eye. A sparring partner's elbow, raised in self-defense as George worked him over with thudding left hooks, did the damage. The cut required stitches and postpone-

ment of the fight. The new date was October 30, 1974, with a starting time of four o'clock in the morning to accommodate closed-circuit television audiences in the United States.

Just as marathon runners are cautioned against wearing new shoes on the day of a race, fight organizers are ill-advised to unveil a new boxing ring on the night of a fight. The Stade du 20 Mai in Zaire's capital city of Kinshasa was unaccustomed to hosting boxing matches. When trainer Angelo Dundee inspected the stadium facilities on the afternoon before the fight, he found that one corner of the ring had sunk into the mud. Concrete slabs were brought in to literally level the playing field.

Other problems remained. The foam rubber padding that had been placed over the ring's wooden underboards was turning to mush in the African humidity. That would slow Ali down. But it wouldn't disadvantage Foreman, who moved ponderously and didn't rely on speed. Also, the turnbuckles holding the ring ropes in place had

★

above FOREMAN WAS THE CHAMPION, BUT ALI RECEIVED TOP BILLING IN THE LOGO FOR THEIR FIGHT.

been tightened to the maximum extent by the workers who erected the ring. That meant the ropes couldn't be further tightened. And because of the heat and humidity, they had started to stretch.

After three minutes of combat against George Foreman, Ali understood two things that he hadn't anticipated in months of visualization and preparation for battle. One: there was no way that he could dance and move effectively on the squishy ring surface. And two: due to the loose ring ropes, there might be some extra room to hide on the perimeter of the ring and thus survive Foreman's blows.

Thus did Ali's genius as a fighter come into play. Under the most crushing pressure imaginable, fueled by imagination and an unshakable belief in himself, he fashioned a new battle plan to use against Foreman.

Leaning against the ropes, Ali pressed his elbows protectively against his sides, placed his opened gloves on his hairline, and awaited Foreman's blows. George consented, turning his body halfway to the right and halfway to the left as he hurled punches that would break most men in half. Peering through his gloves, Ali watched Foreman's shoulders, readied himself for each blow, and leaned back against the ropes to lessen their force or avoid the punches altogether when he could.

Later, Ali referred to this tactic as the "rope-a-dope."

"I didn't really plan what happened that night," he acknowledged. "The ring was slow. Dancing all night,

my legs would have got tired. And George was following me too close, cutting off the ring. In the first round, I used more energy staying away from him than he used chasing me. I was tireder than I should have been with fourteen rounds to go."

"Muhammad's antennas were built to look out for big punches," Foreman explained afterward. "And with the style I had and my tendency to throw big punches, no matter how hard I hit, Muhammad had the instinct to get ready for each punch, ride it through, and be waiting for the next one."

Contrary to legend, the early rounds were not one-sided in Foreman's favor. Fighting off the ropes, Ali won three of the first four stanzas. Rounds five and six belonged to George. But the heat and humidity were taking a toll on the champion. Also, Foreman hadn't been extended past the second round in his most recent eight outings. The middle rounds were unfamiliar territory for him.

By round seven, Foreman was breathing hard. By round eight, his punches had lost their concussive power. As the eighth round drew to a close, Ali slipped off the ropes, caught Foreman with a three-punch combination, and sent him hurtling to the canvas. The fight was over.

Seven years after being unjustly stripped of his title, Muhammad Ali once again was the heavyweight champion of the world.

opposite (top) AFTER OUT-BOXING AND OUT-SMARTING FOREMAN, ALI OUT-SLUGGED HIM.
opposite (bottom) REFEREE ZACK CLAYTON ORDERS ALI TO A NEUTRAL CORNER PRIOR TO BEGINNING THE COUNT THAT WILL END WITH A NEW HEAVYWEIGHT CHAMPION OF THE WORLD.

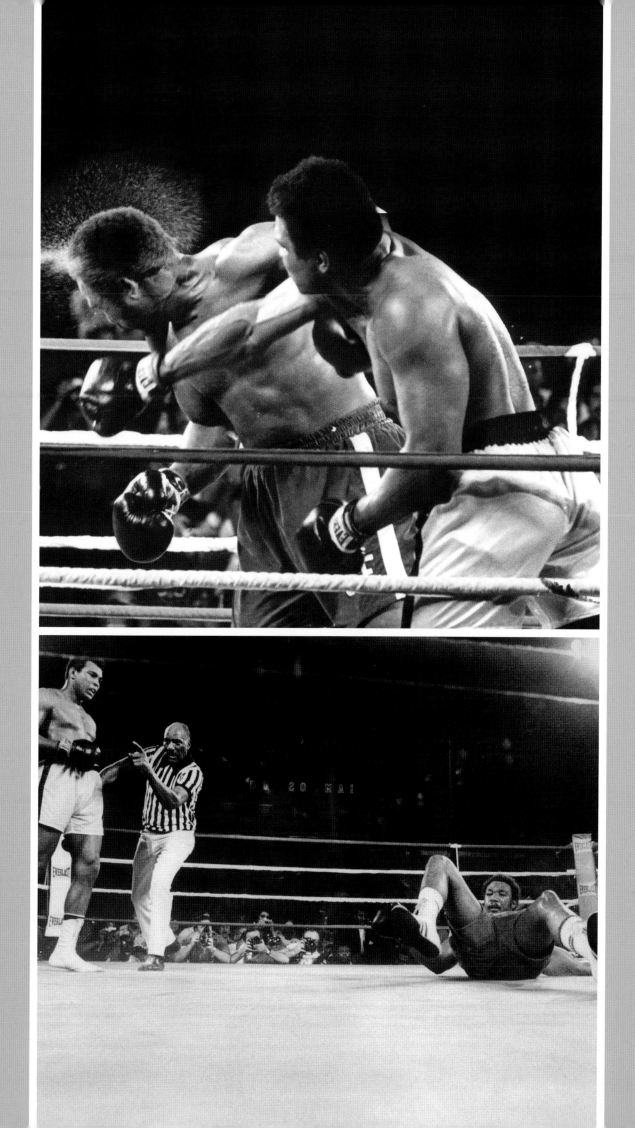

ALI VS. FRAZIER FLYER

Neither man was the champion when Ali and Frazier met for the second time. But Joe had won their first encounter, so his name topped the marquee.

RUMBLE IN THE JUNGLE POSTER

A promotional poster from "The Rumble in the Jungle." Or as Don King put it, "From Slaveship to Championship."

left "ALI BOMAYE!" *opposite* THE ONCE AND FUTURE KING.

THE THRILLA
IN MANILA

"WHAT IT CAME DOWN TO IN MANILA WASN'T THE HEAVY-
WEIGHT CHAMPIONSHIP OF THE WORLD. ALI AND FRAZIER
WERE FIGHTING FOR SOMETHING MORE IMPORTANT THAN
THAT. THEY WERE FIGHTING FOR THE CHAMPIONSHIP OF
EACH OTHER."

—*Jerry Izenberg*

Muhammad Ali's conquest of George Foreman in Zaire made him the most famous and celebrated athlete ever.

Returning to the United States, Ali was accorded near-universal favor. Social views regarding his resistance to the draft had softened. Suspicions about his character had been disproved. His claim to the world's manliest championship was restored. Writers who had once led campaigns against recognizing him as a champion, let alone a hero, sang his praises. And he was as pretty as ever.

At year's end, the Associated Press and *Sports Illustrated* designated Ali as their Athlete of the Year. On December 10, 1974, at the invitation of Gerald Ford, Ali visited the White House. The same man who had been criminally tried and convicted for refusing induction into the United States Army seven years earlier was now an honored

opposite AFTER DEFEATING GEORGE FOREMAN, ALI WAS HONORED WITH
THE S. RAE HICKOK AWARD AS THE 1974 PROFESSIONAL ATHLETE OF
THE YEAR.

guest in the president's home.

Gerald Ford later recalled, "When I took office, we as a nation were pretty much torn apart. There were conflicts between families, in colleges, and on the streets. We'd gone through some serious race problems. The Vietnam War had heightened differences. And of course, there was the heritage of Watergate. One of the major challenges my administration faced was how we could heal the country. Not that everybody had to agree, but at least we should lower our voices and listen to one another. Having Muhammad Ali come to the Oval Office was part of that overall effort. I felt it was important to reach out and indicate individually as well as collectively that we could have honest differences without bitterness."

Asked for his impression of Ali on meeting the champ, Ford said admiringly, "What a hunk of flesh."

In later years, the reach of Ali's celebrity would be referenced many times as a goal for image consultants. But the nature of his celebrity would never be replicated. He was now, truly, "king of the world." Yet he eschewed security details and mingled freely with the masses who approached him. It was an endearing part of his religious faith. "God is my bodyguard," he explained. "Allah watches over me. If I walk into a stadium with a hundred thousand people, no human can keep somebody from putting a bullet in me. But I can't be worrying about things like that. A man filled with fear don't live and enjoy life."

Ali's ease with the media was also unique. Today's celebrities are often cordoned off from the media as much as from their fans. Questions are vetted in advance. Handlers stand ready to stop an interview at the first

above SEVEN YEARS AFTER ALI WAS INDICTED FOR REFUSING TO ACCEPT INDUCTION INTO THE UNITED STATES ARMED FORCES, HE WAS INVITED TO THE WHITE HOUSE AS THE GUEST OF PRESIDENT GERALD FORD.

ALI'S PHYSIQUE AND REMARKABLE RING SKILLS WERE A
PRODUCT OF GENETICS AND TRAINING COMBINED.

MORE THAN ANY FIGHTER EVER, ALI WAS ELEGANCE
PERSONIFIED.

sign of controversy, revoking credentials and suspending access for all but the most sycophantic reporters.

"I don't think there's been an athlete in history who gave as much of himself to the media as Ali," sportswriter Michael Katz later noted. "He worked cooperatively with the media and understood it as well as anyone I've ever known. It wasn't thought out; it came naturally. He liked attention; he knew how to get it; and he accepted writers as part of his world."

On February 25, 1975, two months after Ali visited the White House, Elijah Muhammad died. Elijah had been Ali's most influential spiritual mentor, and his passing saddened Ali. But with his death, the Nation of Islam changed. Elijah's son, Wallace, succeeded his father and

led his followers in a new direction, embracing traditional Islamic values and replacing words of intolerance with professions of love. Some of its ministers, such as Louis Farrakhan, refused to abandon the old teachings. But Ali followed Wallace.

Ali's pronouncements on race were now able to match his actions. Throughout his career, he'd been involved with white people. His most trusted boxing adviser, Angelo Dundee, was a white man of Italian origin. Muhammad had never evinced the hatred that was implicit in Nation of Islam dogma. His first allegiance was to his fellow Muslims, then to black Americans. But he'd never seemed able to reconcile in his mind why love for his own people should manifest itself as hatred toward whites.

above STRETCHING BEFORE A WORKOUT.

The Nation of Islam's overtly racist teachings were the final obstacle that Ali had to overcome to be universally accepted as a hero. Now that dogma was in his past.

ALI-FRAZIER III

After beating George Foreman, Ali took five months off from combat. Next, within the span of ninety-nine days, he defeated Chuck Wepner, Ron Lyle, and Joe Bugner. Then came his historic third bout against Joe Frazier in Manila.

After losing to Ali in their second encounter, Frazier had embarked upon a rehabilitation tour of his own. Still, the prevailing view prior to Ali-Frazier III was that Joe was a spent fighter.

"You have to understand," Ferdie Pacheco later recalled. "The first fight was life and death, and Frazier won. Second fight: Ali figures him out; no problem, relatively easy victory for Ali. Then Ali beats Foreman, and Frazier's sun sets. I don't care what anyone says now; all of us thought that Joe Frazier was shot. We all thought that this was going to be an easy fight. Ali comes out, dances around, and knocks him out in eight or nine rounds."

In the weeks leading up to Ali-Frazier III, Ali donned his carnival barker's hat once more. He was selling the fight and also seeking a psychological edge over his opponent. This time, though, he tarnished himself, even if few recognized it at the time.

Ali had a fondness for giving nicknames to his opponents. In years past, there had been Sonny Liston,

the "Big Ugly Bear" ("Because he's ugly and smells like a bear"); Archie Moore, the "Old Man" ("He's old enough to be my grandfather"); Floyd Patterson, the "Rabbit" ("In the ring, he's frightened like a rabbit"); George Chuvalo, the "Washerwoman" ("He punches like a woman who's washing clothes"); Ernie Terrell, the "Octopus" ("He grabs and holds a lot when he fights"); and George Foreman, the "Mummy" ("George is slow. Clomp! Clomp! He moves like a mummy").

Future fights would see Earnie Shavers, the "Acorn" ("He's got a shaved head that looks like an acorn"); Leon Spinks, "Dracula" ("The man is missing his front teeth"); and Larry Holmes, the "Peanut" ("Because his head is shaped like a peanut").

above WITH PROMOTER DON KING STANDING BETWEEN THEM, ALI AND FRAZIER AGREE TO ONE LAST FIGHT, THIS TIME IN THE PHILIPPINES.

ALI PREFERRED HONING HIS POWER PUNCHES ON THE
HEAVY-BAG IN THE GYM, RATHER THAN BEATING UP ON
SPARRING PARTNERS.

WITH A RUBBER GORILLA IN HIS LEFT BREAST POCKET,
ALI TAUNTS JOE FRAZIER.

For his third encounter with Joe Frazier, Ali labeled his opponent the "Gorilla." At the kick off press conference for the fight, he poetically proclaimed:

> It will be a killer
>
> And a chiller
>
> And a thrilla
>
> When I get the gorilla
>
> In Manila

Then Ali reached into his pocket, pulled out a black rubber gorilla, and told the assembled media, "This here is Joe Frazier's conscience. I keep it everywhere I go. This is the way he looks when you hit him." At which point, Muhammad began pummeling the gorilla and shouting, "All night long, this is what you'll see. Come on, gorilla; we're in Manila. Come on, gorilla; this is a thrilla."

Most of the people in attendance laughed. Frazier was humiliated. Later in the promotion, Ali arranged for someone to wear a black gorilla suit and appear at public workouts.

For five years, Ali had been carrying on about Frazier being "an Uncle Tom, ugly, and ignorant." The gorilla reference went further. Muhammad was a man who traveled the world, telling his followers that he was dedicated to improving the lives of black people. Now, to the glee of mostly white audiences, he was demeaning Frazier with one of the most racist labels imaginable.

There was more at another joint press conference.

"I'm gonna—" Frazier began.

"I'm going to," Ali interrupted. "Not 'I'm gonna.' Talk intelligent."

Frazier went on. "I'm gonna go inta training."

"Not 'inta.' Into. How far did you go in school?"

"As far as you did."

above ALI THROWS A MOCK JAB AT FRAZIER DURING A PRE-FIGHT PRESS CONFERENCE.

"You don't talk that way."

"I hated Ali," Frazier said decades later. "God might not like me talking that way, but it's in my heart."

Ali arrived in the Philippines expecting victory and another coronation. He had a belief in himself and an even larger faith that God would protect him.

Frazier came to the Philippines with faith that was quieter than Ali's, but just as strong. He too believed that he was acting as an instrument of the Almighty; that he had been sent to Manila to humble Ali and show the world that no man was as great as Ali said he was.

What happened in the stultifying heat and humidity of Araneta Coliseum on October 1, 1975, ruined both men physically. It was the most brutal heavyweight championship fight ever.

In the early rounds, Ali had no trouble finding Frazier

with punches. He blasted Joe with fast right hands that followed sharp, stiff jabs; hurting blows. Frazier took unplanned steps backward. But he was as formidable an opponent as he'd ever been. And regardless of the punishment that he took, he would regroup and move forward again.

By the middle rounds, Ali was weakening and his legs were fading. He'd been well trained. But there was no way to prepare for the toll that the heat and Frazier's persistence were taking. Frazier was still coming forward. And now, he was starting to smoke.

Sportswriter Ed Schuyler later recalled, "In round six, Frazier hit Ali with a left hook that's the hardest punch I've ever seen. It had to be harder than the punch he knocked Ali down with in their first fight. Ali's head turned like it was on a swivel, and his response was to look at Frazier and say, 'They told me Joe Frazier was washed up.' And Frazier answered, 'They lied.'"

So it went; round after round. One man would gain an advantage over the other. Then a finishing blow would fail to finish, and the tide would turn again.

Both men were being beaten down. But the punishment that Frazier was absorbing was more visible. Throughout his career, Joe had employed two primary means of defense. The first was a pressing offensive attack that left opponents more concerned with defending themselves than throwing punches. The second was a perpetually moving head. But Frazier's unceasing motion had a pattern that Ali had figured out over the course of

WORLD CHAMPIONSHIP BOUT
Manila, The Philippines
Sept. 30, 1975

	FRAZIER	AGE	ALI
AGE	31		33
WEIGHT	210 lbs.	•	220 lbs.
HEIGHT	5 ft. 11½ in.		6 ft. 3 in.
REACH	73½		80 in.
BICEPS	15½ in.		15 in.
CHEST (Normal)	43 in.		44 in.
CHEST (Expanded)	45 in.		46 in.
WAIST	34½ in.		34 in.
THIGH	26½ in.		26 in.
NECK	18 in.		17½ in.
CALF	15 in.		17 in.

above BOXING'S TRADITIONAL "TALE OF THE TAPE" DOESN'T MEASURE HEART.

REGARDLESS OF THE DEMANDS OF TRAINING, ALI WAS
RARELY TOO BUSY TO VERIFY HIS OWN BEAUTY.

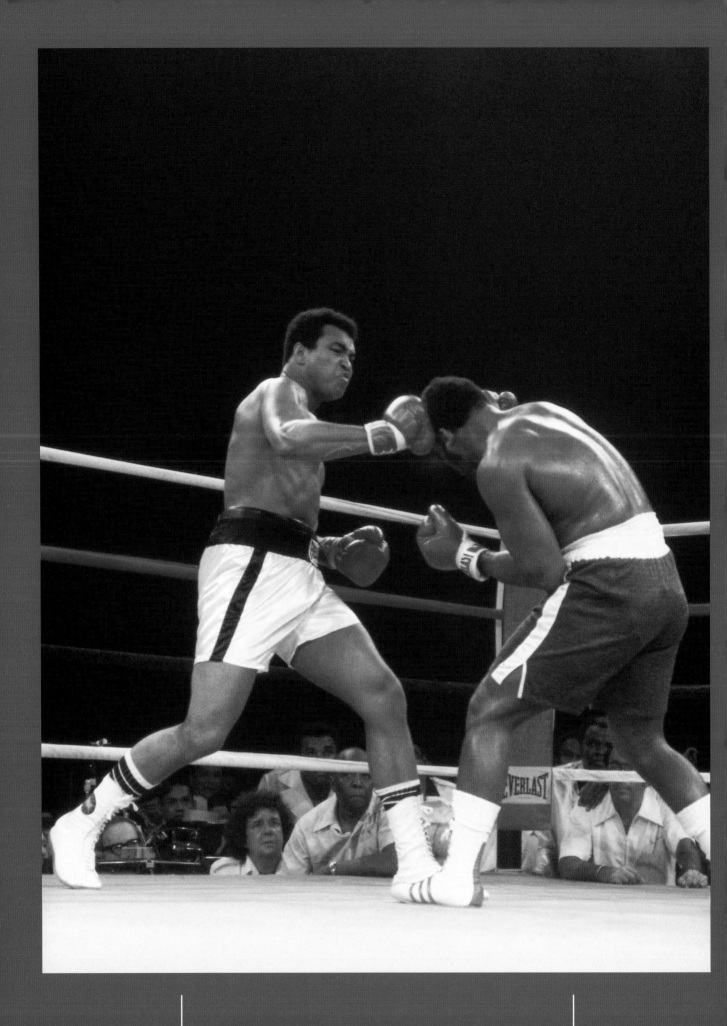

ON OCTOBER 1, 1975, ALI AND FRAZIER CONCLUDED THE
MOST STORIED TRILOGY IN BOXING HISTORY. THIS TIME,
ALI LANDED HIS RIGHT HAND CONSISTENTLY.

their long, brutal rivalry. In Manila, Muhammad knew what he needed to know.

In round fourteen, Ali bludgeoned Frazier again and again, forcing him into a corner. There was no more taunting or talking. Joe kept trying to push forward, but there was no force behind his blows. At the bell ending the round, each man's arms dangled at his sides. Referee Carlos Padilla stepped between them. They were too exhausted to stop leaning on each other.

Ali staggered back to his corner, sank down on his stool, and implored Angelo Dundee to cut his gloves off. He didn't think he could fight any longer. Dundee ignored him and started sponging Muhammad down, getting him ready for the next round.

Frazier wandered toward a point midway along the ring ropes. Padilla directed him to his corner. Joe's mouth was leaking blood.

Eddie Futch, Frazier's trainer, did what he thought had to be done.

"Joe kept getting hit with the right hand," Futch later recalled. "His left eye was completely closed; his right eye was closing. It had been a grueling fight, and that's when fighters get hurt; when they get hit with good, clean punches they don't see and still don't go down. I didn't want Joe's brains scrambled. He had a nice life and a wonderful family to live for. So I decided at the end of the fourteenth round to stop it."

Frazier protested and shook his head weakly.

"No! No, man! No!"

In one understated, elegant gesture, Futch turned toward the referee and unfurled the fingers of his left hand. He would not allow the fight to continue.

Across the ring, Ali realized that the carnage was over. He stood up, lowered his head, and lifted his right glove

above **FRAZIER PRESSED THE ATTACK WITHOUT PAUSE FOR FOURTEEN ROUNDS. BUT IN THE END, IT WASN'T ENOUGH.**

in the air, more in relief than triumph. Then he allowed his body to slowly ooze to the canvas. Later, Muhammad would say that the fight had been "the closest thing to death I know of."

The epic rivalry between Muhammad Ali and Joe Frazier had a less than happy ending. Frazier's anger toward Ali never abated. His emotional scars never healed. The two men never reunited to make friendship tours. But each in his own way has profound respect for the other.

"We were gladiators," Frazier said years later. "I didn't ask no favors of him, and he didn't ask none of me. I don't like him, but I got to say: in the ring he was a man."

"I'm sorry Joe Frazier is mad at me," Ali, for his part, noted. "I'm sorry I hurt him. Joe Frazier is a good man. I couldn't have done what I did without him, and he couldn't have done what he did without me. And if God ever calls me to a holy war, I want Joe Frazier fighting beside me."

above THE PACE IN MANILA WAS UNRELENTING AND BRUTAL. *opposite (top)* PHILIPPINES PRESIDENT FERDINAND MARCOS, DON KING, AND RAHAMAN ALI (MUHAMMAD'S BROTHER) CELEBRATE THE CHAMPION'S VICTORY OVER JOE FRAZIER. *opposite (bottom)* WHENEVER POSSIBLE, PROMOTER DON KING POSITIONED HIMSELF AT ALI'S SIDE.

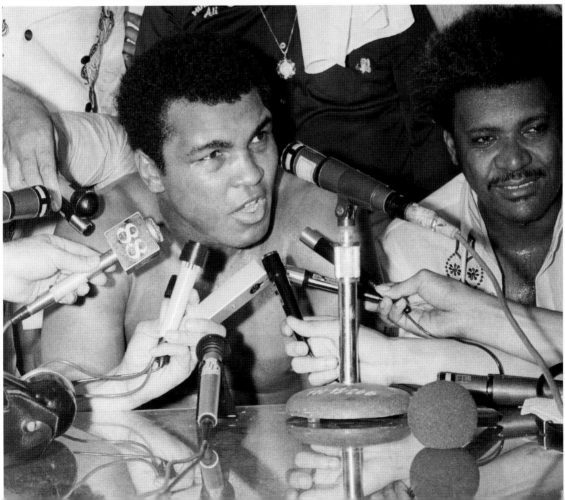

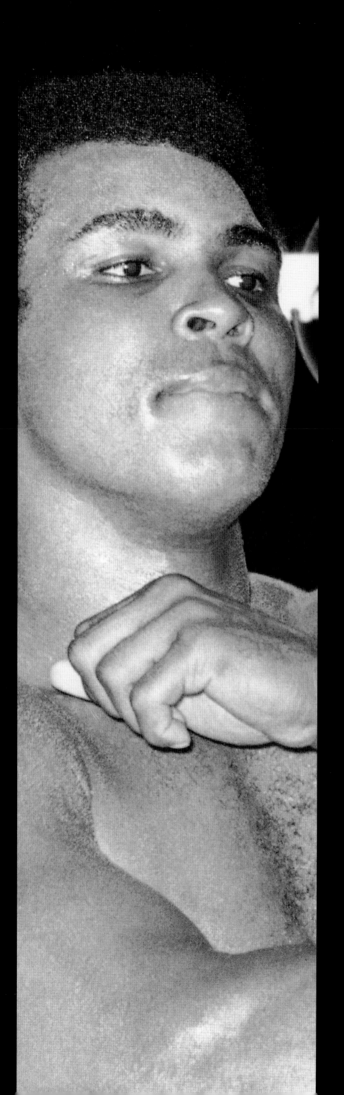

THRILLA IN MANILA PENNANT

A keepsake from the most grueling heavy-weight championship fight ever.

THRILLA IN MANILA FLYER

Promotional flyers for Ali-Frazier III were handed out on the streets of Manila.

left AFTER ALI-FRAZIER III, MUHAMMAD'S LEGACY AS AN ALL-TIME GREAT WAS SOLIDIFIED. BUT HE CHOSE TO FIGHT ON. *opposite* STILL PRETTY AFTER A BATTLE THAT WAS "THE CLOSEST THING TO DEATH I KNOW OF."

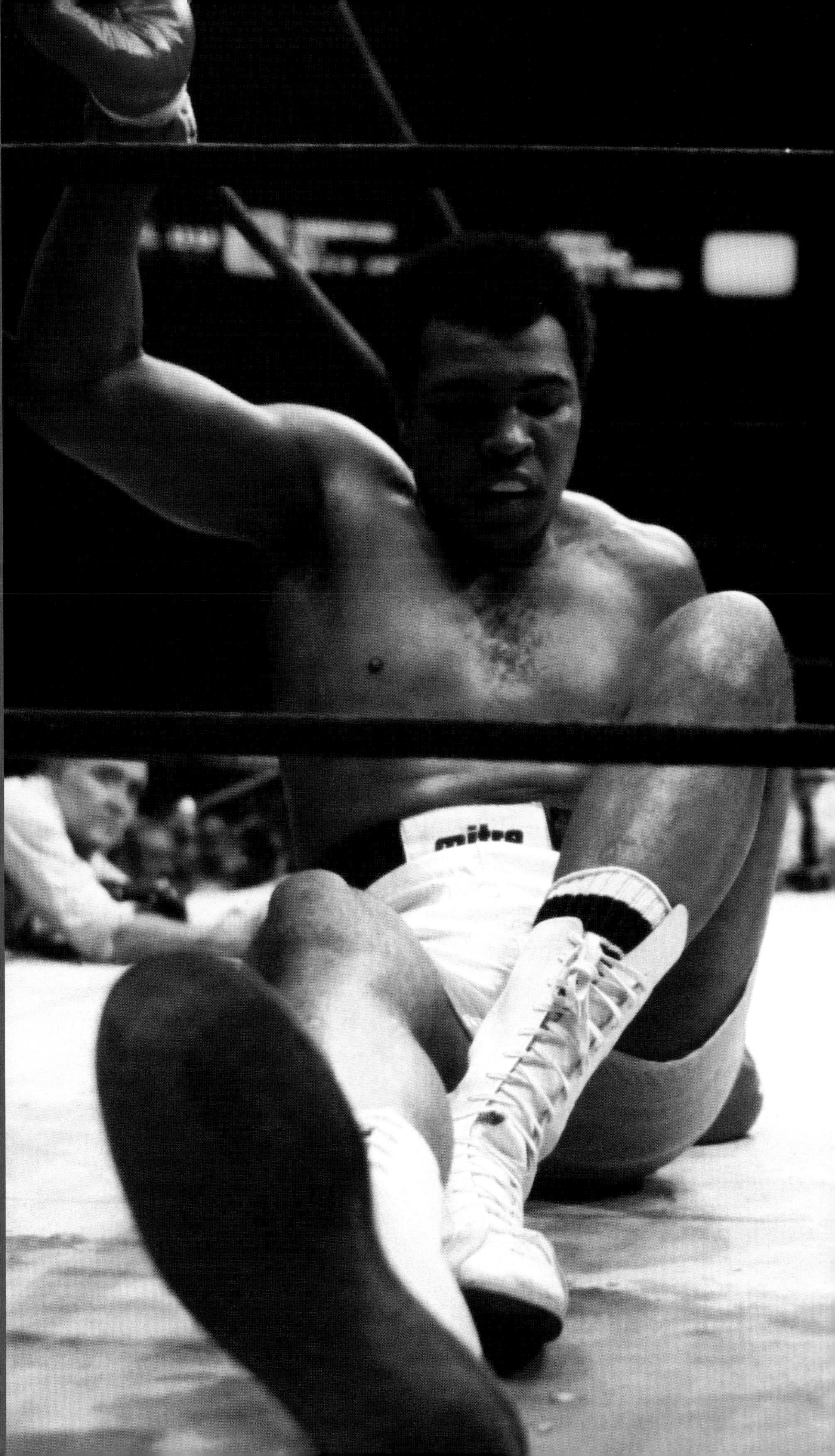

CHAPTER NINE

THE FIGHTER IN DECLINE

"ON FINGER TO NOSE TESTING, THERE IS A SLIGHT DEGREE OF MISSING THE TARGET."

—Dr. Frank Howard, Mayo Clinic Department of Neurology, in his report on a neurological examination of Muhammad Ali conducted prior to Ali fighting Larry Holmes

I f I had to pick a spot to tell him, 'You've got all your marbles, but don't go on anymore,' no question, it would have been after Frazier in Manila. That's when it really started to fall apart."

Thus spoke Ali's ringside physician, Ferdie Pacheco.

Ali returned from Manila adored by the international Muslim community and people of African descent the world over. Eleven countries on four continents took pride in having hosted his fights. He was celebrated in America as a native son. And he was widely regarded as the greatest heavyweight of all time.

Many believe he should have retired. Instead he fought on.

There were lackluster victories in the first five months of 1976 over Jean-Pierre Coopman in Puerto Rico, Jimmy Young in Maryland, and Richard Dunn in Munich. Then Ali took a detour away from boxing to engage in a "mixed martial arts" match

opposite EARNIE SHAVERS COULDN'T PUT MUHAMMAD DOWN WITH HIS PUNCHES. BUT ALI, NO LONGER CATLIKE, SLIPPED TO THE CANVAS IN THE FOURTEENTH ROUND.

against a professional wrestler named Antonio Inoki in Tokyo.

Ali vs. Inoki originally was to have been scripted. Then Muhammad decided that the real thing would be better. The result was an insipid encounter between a man wearing boxing gloves and a man crab-walking around the ring while lying on his back, trying to kick his opponent and refusing to rise from the canvas. The fiasco didn't hurt Ali's legacy as a boxer—it bore no resemblance to boxing—but it didn't help his reputation as an entertainer either. Worse, it inflicted further abuse on his body. Inoki kicked him on the legs again and again. When the travesty was over, Muhammad was hospitalized for the treatment of blood clots.

Ali's next fight—a rubber match against Ken Norton —took place at Yankee Stadium on September 28, 1976. He eked out a close decision victory. Afterward, Mark Kram wrote in *Sports Illustrated*, "There is no question now that Ali is through as a fighter. He threw only one good combination all night. His jab, which once drained and depressed aggression, was only a flick. Only a sure hand on his craft saved him."

There were two fights in 1977. The first was against a club fight–level opponent named Alfredo Evangelista. Ali prevailed over fifteen dreary rounds. Then he stepped into the ring at Madison Square Garden on September 29 to face Earnie Shavers, one of boxing's hardest punchers.

Ali was now thirty-five and reduced to a strategy of

above MUHAMMAD ALI VS. ANTONIO INOKI: A DANGEROUS FARCE.

FAR FROM HIS FIGHTING TRIM, ALI DID HIMSELF
NO FAVORS BY FIGHTING ON AFTER HIS RUBBER MATCH
AGAINST JOE FRAZIER.

AS ALI GREW OLDER AND TRAINED LESS, MORE WEIGHT
ADHERED TO HIS MIDSECTION.

standing with his back against the ropes for long periods of time and taking punishment from men trained in the art of hurting. Permanent damage was being done to his faculties each time he stepped into the ring. But he was surrounded by men whose own livelihood depended upon their ability to keep him feeling good about continuing his career as a fighter.

Ali survived Earnie Shavers, taking enormous punishment but winning a fifteen-round decision.

Then, on February 15, 1978, in Las Vegas, Muhammad fought Leon Spinks.

"NEON LEON"

At the 1976 Montreal Olympics, Leon Spinks had won a gold medal in the light-heavyweight division. Few observers of the boxing scene considered him a threat to Ali's reign. Professionally, "Neon Leon" was a novice with six wins and a draw in seven fights. And he was small for a heavyweight.

"Spinks only has seven fights," Ali told Leon's manager, Butch Lewis, in explaining why he wasn't talking as much as he usually did in promoting the fight. "What am I gonna tell people; that I'm gonna destroy him? Talking that way makes me look stupid."

Little good could come of the fight. Either Spinks would be exposed as an undeveloped fighter or the full extent of Ali's decline would become clear. In the end, there was enough of both to go around.

Ali reported to training camp overweight. Worse,

fifty-seven fights over the course of seventeen years had taken a toll on his willingness to prepare properly for battle. He trained as though he was about to defend his title against an amateur. His primary preoccupation was his weight. As long as the needle on the scale moved closer to his goal, Ali was satisfied. And the yes-men around him assured Ali that he'd never looked better.

Then fight night arrived.

The rope-a-dope didn't work against Spinks. Ali retreated. Leon came forward, punching. Ali covered his face with his hands. Leon kept punching.

Spinks lacked true heavyweight power; but at least he was active. Ali did next to nothing. One sympathetic judge scored the fight in Muhammad's favor by a point.

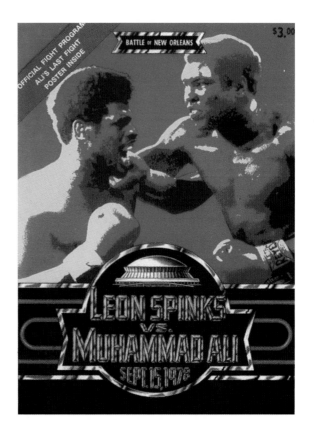

above AFTER AN EMBARRASSING LOSS TO LEON SPINKS, ALI SIGNED FOR A REMATCH, TO BE CONTESTED IN THE LOUISIANA SUPERDOME. THE FIGHT WAS ATTENDED BY 63,315 FANS, THE LARGEST INDOOR CROWD IN THE HISTORY OF AMERICAN BOXING.

The other two judges properly ruled in Spinks's favor.

"Of all the fights I lost in boxing," Muhammad said afterward, "losing to Spinks hurt the most. Leon fought clean; he did the best he could. But it was embarrassing that someone with so little fighting skills could beat me."

Ali pleaded for an immediate rematch and got it. Spinks could make more money fighting Muhammad than any other opponent. But in the interim, Leon was self-destructing. He was undisciplined to begin with. And being heavyweight champion of the world was too strong an intoxicant for him to handle.

"The only person Leon hurts is himself," Butch Lewis said later. "After he won, I had him staying in my apartment. I didn't put him in a hotel because I didn't trust him. Leon told me, 'Butch, you gotta let me go. I need free time. You gotta let me swoop.' So finally, I said, 'Okay, I can't keep you in a cage. I'm gonna be working, setting up endorsements. I'll give you a few days.'"

So Spinks swooped. Then he crashed. A police officer found five dollars' worth of cocaine in his hatband during a routine traffic stop, and Leon was arrested. Images of the heavyweight champion in handcuffs were distributed by wire services around the world.

Then, when it was time for training to begin anew, Spinks was nowhere to be found. "I tracked him down in North Carolina," Lewis later recalled, "in a little shack drinking moonshine whiskey. He's smoking dope, groggier than hell, like this is a dream and he's gonna

above FIGHTING FROM MEMORY IN HIS REMATCH AGAINST SPINKS, ALI HAD JUST ENOUGH LEFT TO WIN.

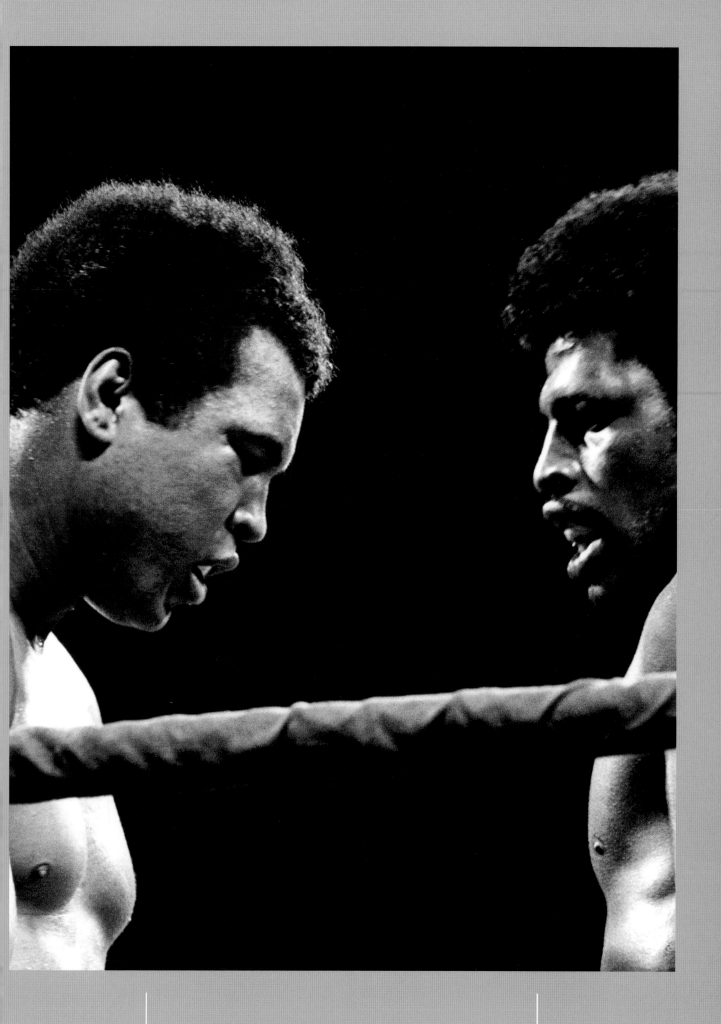

NEEDING TWO TRIES TO BEAT A FIGHTER OF LEON'S CALIBER CONVINCED MUHAMMAD THAT IT WAS TIME TO RETIRE.

MUHAMMAD ALI TAKES A DEXTERITY TEST AFTER HIS
FIRST RETIREMENT FROM BOXING.

enjoy it because any day he might wake up. At most, he trained ten days for the rematch."

Meanwhile, Ali was training with a vengeance, hoping to win the heavyweight title for an unprecedented third time. On September 15, 1978, he fashioned a unanimous fifteen-round decision triumph. It was a slow, boring fight. Muhammad's strategy was to jab, jab again, throw occasional right hands, and tie Spinks up whenever the smaller man worked his way inside.

"Forget all that stuff about Ali going back and working hard and being better the second time around," Lewis said later. "Ali wasn't better the second time against Leon. Ali was worse. Ali had slipped even more than before, but Leon went against him with nothing at all."

On June 26, 1979, nine months after defeating Leon Spinks, Ali announced his retirement from boxing.

"Everybody gets old," he told reporters. "I'd be a fool to fight again."

THE FIRST RETIREMENT

Professional athletes tend to grow restless after they retire. They've been accustomed to adulation of a certain kind that, suddenly, is no longer there. Ali intended to be as different from the norm in retirement as he had been in boxing. After all, he'd starred on Broadway in a play called *Buck White* in 1969 and in a television miniseries called *Freedom Road* ten years later. He'd been a guest at the White House and met with Leonid Brezhnev, the leader of the Soviet Union. He'd been in the forefront of America's cultural revolution and drawn enormous crowds wherever he went.

He was Muhammad Ali.

★

above WEARING A SUIT AND TIE INSTEAD OF TRUNKS AND GLOVES, ALI TRIED TO MAKE THE TRANSITION FROM BOXER TO BUSINESSMAN.

Then Ali's self-image took a hit.

In December 1979, the Soviet Union invaded Afghanistan. In response, at the urging of President Jimmy Carter, the United States Olympic Committee announced that the United States would boycott the 1980 Moscow Olympics. The White House then began working through diplomatic channels to gather support for the boycott from other nations.

"One of the things I did in that regard," Jimmy Carter later recalled, "was ask the most famous person in our country to represent me and the government of the United States in Africa. There was a specific interest on my part in having Muhammad Ali explain our country's position on the Olympic boycott."

Having met with numerous world leaders in the past, Ali believed that he was suited for the art of diplomacy. He sometimes referred to himself as "the black Henry Kissinger." In reality, he was no more capable of representing the United States as a diplomat than Henry Kissinger was of defending himself in a boxing ring. Yet government officials who should have known better tossed Muhammad into the middle of the Olympic boycott controversy.

Ali was flattered and answered his country's call. He went first to Tanzania. Tanzanian officials were not flattered. "Would the United States send Chris Evert to negotiate with London?" one of them demanded.

Worse, Ali was wholly unprepared for his mission. Upon learning that the United States had refused a request by twenty-nine African countries to join a boycott

---

★

above AT JIMMY CARTER'S REQUEST, ALI SOUGHT AFRICAN SUPPORT FOR A BOYCOTT OF THE 1980 MOSCOW OLYMPICS IN RESPONSE TO THE SOVIET UNION'S INVASION OF AFGHANISTAN.

ALI'S DIPLOMATIC MISSION TO AFRICA DID NOT GO WELL.

ONCE MORE TO THE WELL; THIS TIME, TO FIGHT
LARRY HOLMES.

of the 1976 Montreal Olympics because the apartheid nation of South Africa had been invited, Muhammad told his Tanzanian hosts, "They didn't tell me about that in America. Maybe I'm being used to do something that ain't right. You're making me look at things different."

Awkward stops in Kenya, Liberia, and Senegal followed. *Time* magazine described the tour as "the most bizarre diplomatic mission in recent U.S. history."

Talk of a comeback began as soon as Ali returned home. What better way to restore his stature as a great man than to win the heavyweight championship for a fourth time?

ALI VS. LARRY HOLMES

In Muhammad Ali's absence from boxing, Larry Holmes had ascended to the heavyweight throne.

Holmes, once an Ali sparring partner, was a great fighter in the making. Las Vegas knew a mega-event when it saw one. A temporary arena that seated 24,000 fans was constructed in the parking lot at Caesars Palace.

But there were rumors about Ali's physical condition and his thickening tongue. The Nevada State Athletic Commission needed a fig leaf to cover itself before it granted Ali a license to box. That cover came from a visit by Muhammad to the Mayo Clinic in Minnesota for a renal and neurological examination.

Thereafter, the members of the Nevada commission appeared to be too busy waving the Mayo Clinic report in the air to actually read it. Or maybe they read it and decided that the Las Vegas economy would be better served if the contents of the report weren't revealed.

A decade later, the report was made public. In it, Dr. Frank Howard of the Mayo Clinic Department of Neurology noted that Muhammad was tired on the day

above THE SPIRIT WAS WILLING, BUT THE FLESH WAS WEAK.

of the examination and then wrote that Ali told him he had been "dazed on two occasions" during the course of his professional boxing career.

In truth, Ali had been punched in the head thousands of times by sparring partners and ring opponents trained in the art of beating a man senseless. Dr. Howard might not have understood that. Certainly, the powers that be at the Nevada State Athletic Commission did. But that red flag regarding the credibility of the Mayo Clinic report paled in comparison to what followed.

"The remainder of his examination is normal," the report continued, "except that he does not quite hop with the agility that one might anticipate; and on finger to nose

testing, there is a slight degree of missing the target."

Missing the target of one's nose with an index finger? That would call an application for a driver's license into question, let alone a license to fight for the heavyweight championship of the world.

Thereafter, while refusing to make the report public, the Nevada State Athletic Commission cited it as justification for licensing Ali to fight Larry Holmes.

Then matters got worse. Several weeks before the fight, Ali was well over his fighting weight. Dr. Charles Williams, a physician who treated him from time to time, decided on the basis of Muhammad's appearance that he was suffering from a hypothyroid condition. The diagnosis was speculative and incorrect. Nonetheless, Williams prescribed Thyrolar to treat it.

"If a fighter needs Thyrolar," Ferdie Pacheco, who was no longer with Ali, said later, "it's like Russian roulette for him to be in the ring. His heart rate accelerates. His basic metabolism changes. His muscles are affected, because muscle tissue as well as fat is burning off. He's debilitated by loss of water. He can't sweat. Ali was a walking time bomb in the ring that night. He could have had anything from a heart attack to a stroke to all kinds of bleeding in the head."

But from Ali's point of view, the Thyrolar was working. After two weeks, his body was trim again. He loved what he saw when he looked in the mirror.

Even veteran sportswriters were fooled. "Whatever happens when Ali meets Larry Holmes," Pat Putnam

above ALI APPROACHED HIS FIGHT AGAINST LARRY HOLMES BELIEVING HE HAD A CREDIBLE CHANCE TO WIN THE HEAVYWEIGHT CHAMPIONSHIP FOR AN UNPRECEDENTED FOURTH TIME.

AS ALI-HOLMES DREW NEAR, MUHAMMAD STRUGGLED TO
REGAIN HIS FIGHTING PHYSIQUE. HERE, HE ADDRESSES
AN OPEN-WORKOUT CROWD, THE LINES OF HIS BACK
SMOOTH AND SOFT.

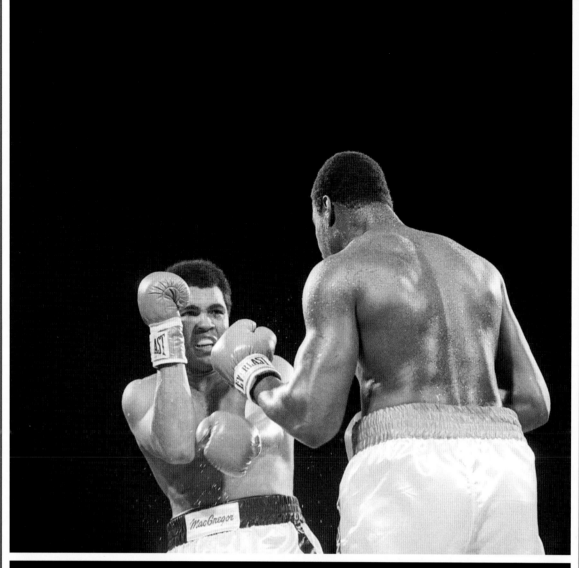

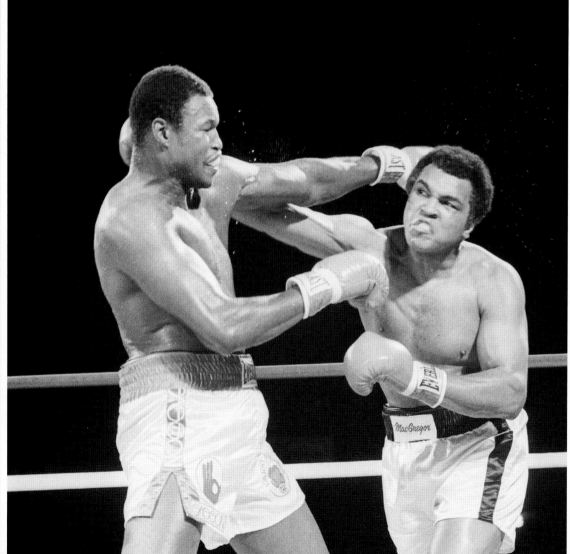

wrote, "One irrefutable fact will stand out. Ali will be in better physical and mental condition than at any time since he battled George Foreman. His face is slim and firm. So is his body. It's as if he has turned the clock back to 1971, when he was twenty-nine."

Fighters tend to believe that they're invincible. For so long as they make a living in prizefighting, they don't want to imagine otherwise. "I've never been beaten," the undefeated fighter says. "I've never been seriously hurt," the fighter with several losses on his record offers. "I've never been knocked out," the journeyman with as many losses as wins tells himself. "It only hurts for a minute," says the trial horse who has been bludgeoned unconscious multiple times.

On October 2, 1980, Muhammad Ali walked across the parking lot at Caesars Palace and climbed several steps into a boxing ring to do battle against Larry Holmes. Sylvester Stallone, who was at ringside, later likened the brutality that followed to "an autopsy on a man who's still alive."

The young Ali had been virtually untouchable. The two hardest punchers he faced prior to his exile from boxing were Sonny Liston and Cleveland Williams. There was no clowning around in those fights. In the first Liston fight, discounting the round when Ali was temporarily blinded, Liston hit him with less than a dozen punches per round, most of them jabs. In the second Liston fight, Liston landed only two punches. When Ali fought Cleveland Williams, Williams hit him a total of three times.

Time goes by. A fighter grows old.

In Manila, Joe Frazier landed 440 punches. In

opposite (top) **FOR MOST OF THE NIGHT, LARRY HOLMES WAS ON THE OFFENSIVE.** *opposite (bottom)* **ALI'S PUNCHES WERE FEW AND FAR BETWEEN. AND MOST OF THEM MISSED.** *above* **AFTER TEN UGLY ROUNDS, ALI-HOLMES WAS STOPPED. HOLMES WON EVERY ROUND ON EACH JUDGE'S SCORECARD.**

THE FIGHTER IN DECLINE

LISTON	PATTERSON	CHUVALO	COOPER	LONDON
MILDENBERGER	WILLIAMS	TERRELL	FOLLEY	QUARRY
BONAVENA	FRAZIER	NORTON	FOREMAN	WEPNER
LYLE	BUGNER	COOPMAN	YOUNG	DUNN

Muhammad's first fight against Leon Spinks, Spinks connected 482 times.

Larry Holmes battered Ali with 320 head-snapping, gut-wrenching, punishing blows. One hundred twenty-five of those punches landed in the ninth and tenth rounds when Muhammad was unable to defend himself and Holmes was throwing everything he had.

The fight was stopped by Angelo Dundee after ten one-sided rounds; far too late for the stoppage to be called merciful.

Ali would fight one more time. On December 11, 1981, he lost a ten-round decision to Trevor Berbick in the Bahamas. Berbick wouldn't have won one minute of one round against Ali when Muhammad was in his prime.

The next day, once and for all, Ali retired from boxing. "Father Time caught up with me," he told the media at a press conference. "I'm finished. I've got to face the facts. I know it's the end. I'm not crazy. We all grow old."

above TWENTY OF THE MEN ALI FOUGHT IN WORLD-CHAMPIONSHIP CONTESTS.

THE MOST FAMOUS NAME IN BOXING HISTORY, AND
PERHAPS ALL SPORTS HISTORY.

ALI VS. NORTON POSTER

The rubber match between Ali and Ken Norton was the first time that they faced each other in a championship fight.

ALI VS. HOLMES TICKET

Holmes-Ali was Muhammad's last appearance in a championship bout, and fight fans shelled out big bucks to see him.

left ALI FOUGHT ON, WELL PAST HIS PHYSICAL PRIME. *opposite* THREE GRUELING FIGHTS AGAINST KEN NORTON CONTRIBUTED TO MUHAMMAD'S DECLINE.

CHAPTER TEN

THE
OLYMPIC
FLAME

"STILL EXUDING NOBILITY AND STATURE; AND THE RESPONSE HE EVOKES IS PART AFFECTION, PART EXCITEMENT, BUT ESPECIALLY RESPECT."

—Bob Costas

S oon after Muhammad Ali retired from boxing, rumors of his deteriorating physical condition began to proliferate. There were denials. Sure, Ali had endured some tough rounds in the latter part of his ring career. But how could a man so handsome and physically imposing, still bursting with energy and willing to make personal appearances around the world, possibly be considered sick?

"If that's what sick looks like," the denials went, "we should all be so sick."

Some of the denials came from Ali. It was hard enough when his body had failed him as an athlete. But for it to fail him as an everyday man?

Still, by 1984, it was clear that Muhammad was suffering from something more than the normal aging process that comes to all men and women. His words were no longer as audible as they'd once been. His balance was poor. "Nobody in the history of boxing took a better punch than Muhammad Ali," Hugh McIlvanney wrote. "Sadly, there's a price to be paid for that."

opposite WHEN ALI RETIRED AS AN ACTIVE FIGHTER, HE STILL HAD THE PRETTIEST SMILE IN BOXING AND A TWINKLE IN HIS EYE.

THE PHYSICAL DECLINE

Ali entered the Columbia-Presbyterian Medical Center in New York for diagnostic tests in September 1984. He downplayed the visit when talking to reporters. "I'm in no pain," he said. "Sometimes, I have trembling in my hands. My speech is slurred. People say to me, 'What did you say? I can't understand you.' I'm not scared, but my family and friends are."

After eight days of tests, Ali's supervising physician, Dr. Stanley Fahn, issued a statement that read in part, "Muhammad Ali does not have Parkinson's disease. Ali exhibits some mild symptoms of Parkinson's syndrome."

In making that distinction, Dr. Fahn was saying that Ali had the symptoms of Parkinson's disease, but that these symptoms had a different cause. Five years later, with Muhammad's permission, Dr. Fahn added to the record, noting, "At the time, he requested that I not state publicly what in my view was the cause of his Parkinsonism. My assumption is that his physical condition resulted from repeated blows to the head."

"I don't want anyone to feel sorry for me, because I had a good life before and I'm having a good life now," Ali said thereafter. "My problem with speaking bothers other people more than it bothers me."

above URGED BY FAMILY MEMBERS AND FRIENDS TO HAVE A MEDICAL EVALUATION, ALI UNDERWENT DIAGNOSTIC TESTS THAT REVEALED THE ONSET OF PARKINSON'S SYNDROME. *opposite* FOR DECADES, A FLOOD OF FAN MAIL HAS ARRIVED DAILY AT ALI'S DOOR.

It bothered other people a lot. For decades, Ali had been an international figure who spoke to and for the world's silent and oppressed masses. He'd given voice to the supervening issues of equality, war, and civil rights. He was animated. His beautiful features sparkled. His charismatic smile disarmed even those who did not share his views. Now his voice was fading and his face sometimes seemed to be a lifeless mask.

"Muhammad was what people wanted him to be for so many years that it's hard for them to accept the fact that he isn't that way anymore," his wife Lonnie said. "People tried in good faith to explain away the situation by saying, 'Muhammad is bored; Muhammad is tired.

Muhammad is fine; he's just a little depressed.' And those people might have been trying to help, but the truth is, Muhammad does have a physical problem."

WIVES AND CHILDREN

Lonnie Ali is Muhammad's fourth wife. Ali married for the first time at age twenty-two, between his first and second fights against Sonny Liston. His bride was a cocktail waitress and former model named Sonji Roi, who took and later kept the name Sonji Clay. She did not fit the Nation of Islam profile for a Muslim wife.

"Most of the Muslims didn't like her," Jerry Izenberg, the dean of American sportswriters, later noted. "She

opposite (top) CASSIUS CLAY'S FIRST WIFE, SONJI, WAS ALSO HIS FIRST TRUE LOVE. *opposite (bottom)* ALI AND HIS SECOND WIFE, BELINDA. *above* AFTER NINE YEARS OF MARRIAGE, MUHAMMAD AND BELINDA WENT SEPARATE WAYS.

wouldn't wear the veil and headdress, and she asked questions that maybe they didn't want asked."

Ali and Sonji were divorced in early 1966 after less than two years of marriage. Nineteen months later, Ali married again, this time to a seventeen-year-old Muslim woman named Belinda Boyd. Raised by strict Islamic parents, she was dutifully subservient in public as Ali's wife and the mother of their four children. But she showed private strength in shepherding him through the most difficult years of his professional life, those spent in exile from boxing.

"The government had taken away his title, and we thought boxing was gone forever," Belinda later recalled. "We didn't have much money, but we said, 'It don't matter; we're gonna make it.' I didn't need money for my clothes. I sewed my own; I was trained that way. We did without and we worked together. It was good; me and Ali."

But there came a time when Ali chose to stray repeatedly outside his marriage. And before his third fight against Joe Frazier in Manila, his private life erupted into a scandal. Veronica Porche was a twenty-one-year-old model when Ali met her during prefight promotion

above IN 1977, AFTER ALI AND BELINDA WERE DIVORCED, HE MARRIED VERONICA PORCHE.

MUHAMMAD AND VERONICA HAD TWO DAUGHTERS
DURING THEIR NINE-YEAR MARRIAGE.

IN 1986, ALI MARRIED LONNIE WILLIAMS, WHO HAD
KNOWN HIM SINCE CHILDHOOD.

for his 1974 battle against George Foreman. She was one of four women selected to appear on a poster that advertised the fight and later traveled to Zaire to be available for Muhammad. She and Ali saw one another often during the following year.

In Manila, Ali brought Veronica to a reception at the presidential palace, where they met Philippine president Ferdinand Marcos. An article recounting details of the encounter was published soon after in *Newsweek* magazine. The next day, at a press conference, Ali told the media, "I could see some controversy if she was white, but she's not. The only person I answer to is Belinda Ali, and I don't worry about her."

Twenty-four hours later, Belinda was on a plane to Manila. She angrily confronted Muhammad in his hotel room and returned to the United States immediately thereafter. The following March, Ali's first child with Veronica—Hana Ali—was born. On September 2, 1976, Belinda filed for divorce.

Ali and Veronica married in 1977. They had a second daughter, Laila, who, for a time, followed in her father's footsteps as a professional boxer.

"I thought that we could have a normal life if he wasn't in boxing," Veronica said years later. "I was very naïve back then. We never could have had a normal life because he'd still be Muhammad Ali."

In 1986, Ali and Veronica were divorced. Later that year, Muhammad married Lonnie Williams, who had been raised in a house across the street from his parents' home.

"I met Muhammad when I was five-and-a-half," Lonnie later said. "There's something I have in my relationship with Muhammad that his other wives didn't have. I've known him for so long that I have a little better sense of who he is and where he comes from."

Much of the fortune that Ali accumulated during his ring career was spent on an excessive entourage or given away. Some went to former wives and for the support of eight children, including two born to women whom Muhammad never married. Long after his fighting days were over, Muhammad and Lonnie adopted another child together.

★

above ALI POSES WITH HIS DAUGHTER LAILA, WHO COMPILED A 24–0 RECORD WITH 21 KNOCKOUTS DURING HER SEVEN YEARS OF PRIZEFIGHTING.

Another portion of Ali's money was stolen outright by people that he trusted. "It didn't take a genius to hustle Ali," said Gene Dibble, an investment advisor to Muhammad in the 1970s. "I've never seen a man who made so much money, tried to make so much money, and at the same time had such tremendous disregard for money."

In 1978, a team of financial and legal advisors put together at the behest of the chief executive officer of First National Bank of Chicago sought to right Ali's finances. The International Management Group, better known as IMG, was brought into the fold in the hope that it would market Muhammad's name, image, and likeness as successfully as it had marketed those of golfer Arnold Palmer. But by then, too many hustlers had their hooks in Ali. Eventually, the team of advisers disbanded.

Meanwhile, as his physical condition continued to worsen, Ali spent less and less time in the spotlight. He was still universally loved. He drew crowds wherever he went. But did he still matter?

THE ATLANTA OLYMPICS

Fifteen years after his final performance as a fighter, Ali answered that question. On July 19, 1996, he lit the Olympic flame at the twenty-sixth Olympiad in Atlanta.

above MUHAMMAD AND LONNIE WITH THEIR SON, ASAAD, NOW NINETEEN YEARS OLD.
opposite DECADES AFTER HIS LAST PRIZEFIGHT, ALI REMAINS THE MOST RECOGNIZABLE PERSON IN THE WORLD.

THIRTY-SIX YEARS AFTER WINNING A GOLD MEDAL
IN ROME, ALI LIT THE OLYMPIC FLAME AT THE 1996
ATLANTA OLYMPICS.

Ali's selection had been kept secret from the public until the moment the torch was handed to him. NBC commentators Bob Costas and Dick Enberg described the entrance of the torch into Olympic Stadium, carried by former world heavyweight champion Evander Holyfield, an Olympic bronze medalist raised in Atlanta.

Olympic swimmer Janet Evans received the torch from Holyfield and carried it up through the stands toward the cauldron.

Then Ali emerged from the shadows.

Evans handed the torch to the man who, as a precocious eighteen-year-old, had won an Olympic gold medal in Rome.

The stadium erupted in applause.

With hundreds of millions of people around the world watching and the spotlight again upon him, Ali raised the torch above his head. His left hand shook at his waist, but his right arm held steady.

"Still a great, great presence," Costas proclaimed. "Still exuding nobility and stature, and the response he evokes is part affection, part excitement, but especially respect."

Ali leaned forward and lit the fuse that carried the flame upward to the cauldron.

"What a moment!"

★

above **"LOOK AT MY FACE. STILL PRETTY."**

CHAPTER ELEVEN

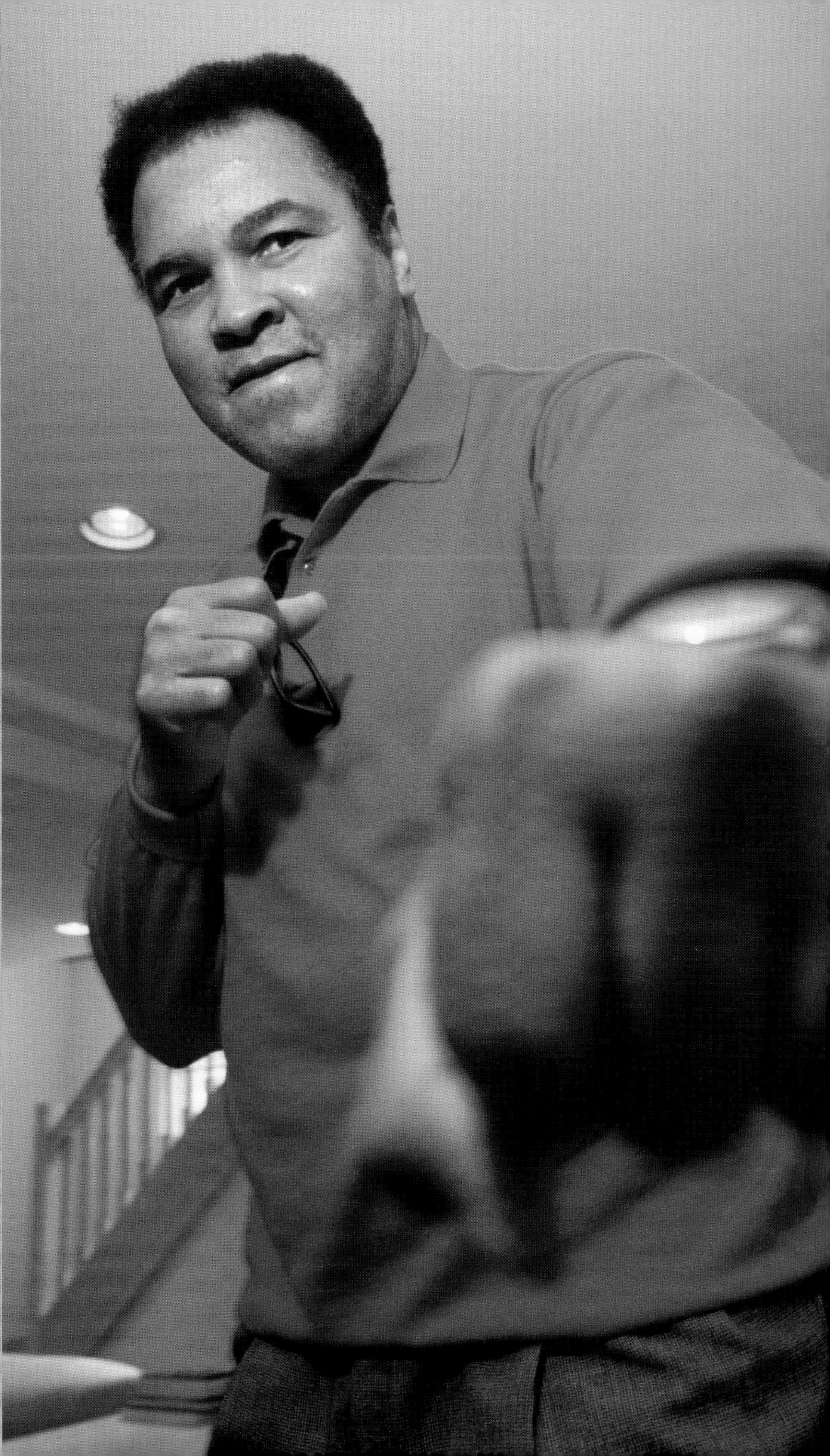

A WARRIOR
AT PEACE

"THERE WILL ALWAYS BE ANOTHER GREAT FIGHTER. THERE WILL ALWAYS BE ANOTHER GREAT BASEBALL PLAYER. BUT THERE WILL NEVER BE ANOTHER MUHAMMAD ALI."
—*Bryant Gumbel*

The early years of Muhammad Ali's retirement, like much of his time in boxing, were marked by the inability to say "no." Whole books could be filled with anecdotes about his limitless generosity to charities and individuals less fortunate than himself. He lived with the same openness that marked his public appearances when he was heavyweight champion of the world—no security detail, no fear of anyone wishing him harm—and opened his home to anyone who knocked on his door. But as his health continued to deteriorate and his means of earning a living diminished, some protective boundaries had to be established.

In the years after Ali lit the Olympic flame in Atlanta, his wife Lonnie, who has a master's degree in business administration, became the primary caretaker of his legacy and finances. Soon, legacy and finance were intertwined. The generation that controlled corporate America had grown up admiring Ali in their formative years. Thus, his legacy had the potential to become a lucrative venture. But first, it was deemed

opposite MUHAMMAD ALI AT HOME IN BERRIEN SPRINGS, MICHIGAN: "IF YOU EVEN DREAM OF BEATING ME, YOU BETTER WAKE UP AND APOLOGIZE."

desirable to edit history a bit in order to take full advantage of Muhammad's economic potential. Many of the rough edges attached to his life story—references to "white devils" and the like—were filed away.

"Commercialization is a natural process in this country," Jerry Izenberg observed. "But the Ali I fell in love with wasn't for sale. He fought the good fight in and out of the ring, and that was payment enough for him. The true worth of the stands he made wasn't commercial."

Corporate America's redefining of Ali continued with the 2001 feature film *Ali* that starred Will Smith and cost the staggering sum of $105,000,000 to bring to the screen. The film sought to further reshape Muhammad's image, scrubbing it of the verbal attacks he'd made on Frazier, softening the Nation of Islam's racist teachings, and reducing Ali's promiscuity to a single extramarital affair.

Ali faced criticism for being answerable in part to corporate schedules and corporate revenue projections. He was less inclined to offer political thoughts that might ruffle feathers.

"I've opened up businesses across the country, selling products," Ali told journalist David Frost in June 2002 when asked about al-Qaeda. "I don't want to say nothing and, not knowing what I'm doing, not [being] qualified, say the wrong thing and hurt my businesses."

above ALI MUGS WITH ACTOR WILL SMITH AS PART OF THE PROMOTION FOR THE 2001 MOVIE *ALI.*

ALI RECEIVING *SPORTS ILLUSTRATED'S* SPORTSMAN OF
THE CENTURY AWARD ON DECEMBER 2, 1999.

On April 11, 2006, the licensing firm CKX, Inc., announced that it had paid Ali fifty million dollars to acquire an 80 percent interest in, and control over, his name, image, likeness, and other rights of publicity.

While some criticized Ali for selling out, he continued to support charitable causes. Meanwhile, the eighty-four-million-dollar Muhammad Ali Center opened in Ali's hometown of Louisville the year before. Created to advance the ideals of "respect, confidence, conviction, dedication, giving, and spirituality," the Ali Center has hosted events as diverse as Martin Luther King Jr. Day celebrations and a naturalization ceremony for new United States citizens. Fundraising continues for Phase Two of the Center, which its board of directors says will be comprised of "permanent exhibits that focus on finding personal greatness."

It's generally acknowledged that Ali's greatest impact upon society came in the 1960s, when his conduct bordered on revolutionary and he was at his most controversial. Much of his life since the 1996 Atlanta Olympics has been an extended victory lap of sorts.

Meanwhile, a new generation of Americans is taking its own look at Ali. Some in this generation are distrustful of the transformation of athletes into global brands. Others style themselves as political conservatives. Often, they focus on that part of the man who joined a black-separatist movement when he was young, embraced segregation of the races for a decade, and treated several other black athletes with a startling degree of cruelty. This new generation questions whether Ali is deserving of the adulation that he receives. They wonder if Ali's generation loved him while understanding his flaws,

opposite (top) IN 2005, THE MUHAMMAD ALI CENTER OPENED IN LOUISVILLE, KENTUCKY. *opposite (bottom)* ALI WITH HIS WIFE, LONNIE, AND DAUGHTERS JAMILLA (LEFT) AND RASHEEDA (SECOND LEFT) AT THE DEDICATION OF THE ALI CENTER. *above* ALI, WITH MUSTACHE, REFERRED TO HIMSELF AS "DARK GABLE."

or if they found him on a treasure hunt for rebellious figurines.

In response, it should first be acknowledged that Ali faltered at times. But he took as long a view of his role in society as any superstar ever. His was not a faux rebellion, but a number of unpopular stands that came with extremely adverse consequences for himself.

Ali gave up the heavyweight championship of the world for what he believed in. He was sentenced to five years in prison, not for a drug-related crime or an incident of domestic abuse, but for a principled stand against a war that he thought was immoral. He sacrificed a fortune in endorsement income when he was young; a fortune that no contemporary athlete would forsake.

His successors, by contrast, act at times as though they see nothing so immoral as being stripped of an apparel maker's logo.

There's no end to credible testimony about Ali's goodness. He touched people the world over with his warmth and love. Both literally and metaphorically, he has kissed without hesitation the poor and weak, the downtrodden and oppressed, the elderly and sick, and everyone else he met.

New generations must rely in part on the testimony of those who lived through Ali's glory years. Then, one hopes, they will understand both Ali's legacy and the legacy of Ali's generation.

Some see an inconsistency in celebrating a man as a

above THOUGH NO LONGER FIGHTING, ALI'S LIFE STILL CENTERS ON THE BOXING RING.

MUHAMMAD ALI AND FORMER PRESIDENT BILL CLINTON:
TWO WARRIORS EMBRACE.

THE CHILDREN IN THIS PHOTO ARE TEENAGERS NOW,
BUT, DOUBTLESS, THEY STILL REMEMBER MEETING ALI.

messenger of love when he rose to fame by bludgeoning others with his fists. But history teaches that warriors often become pacifists if given enough years to live. A man who has felt the weight of violence frequently seeks to shield others from it. And because an old warrior's courage cannot be questioned, he can be an ideal spokesperson for peace.

Ali today lives in serenity. Behind a face that no longer expresses itself as it once did, his mind and spirit still pursue ideals that are dear to his heart. He meant so much to so many people. More than anyone else of his generation, he built himself into a ubiquitous presence and embodied the most heroic impulses of others. People around the world—whether by virtue of their race, religion, nationality, or principles—looked at him and saw their best selves reflected back. He allowed others to bask in the glow of his courage and accomplishments as though these things were their own.

"Without Ali, life would have been good," Jimmy Ellis once said. "But it was a lot better because of him."

Journalist and political activist Mike Marqusee has written, "The greatest lesson of Muhammad Ali's life and career is his rejection of a narrow American national identity in favor of a personal identity that crosses all borders and sees the individual as part of a global community that is diverse, but also united in its essential humanity."

That said, it should be noted that Ali is uniquely American. In no other country and at no other time could the phenomenon of Muhammad Ali have flowered as it did. The civil rights and antiwar movements of the 1960s were there for him to flow into. He wouldn't have had

above ALI RECEIVES THE HIGHEST HONOR PRESENTED BY THE NATIONAL ASSOCIATION OF BROADCASTERS EDUCATION FOUNDATION IN RECOGNITION OF HIS COMMITMENT TO WORLD PEACE.

the same impact without them. And the United States afforded him the environment in which he could go beyond the norms of established protest and make his stands. As misguided as his allegiance to the Nation of Islam might have been, as unjustifiable as his refusal to be inducted into the United States Army was in the eyes of many, Ali would not have survived those confrontations with authority had he made them in most nations of the world.

The one part of Ali's legacy that no one questions, of course, is his legacy as the greatest fighter of his time, and perhaps the greatest of all time. Ali fought every challenger and got up from every knockdown. In winning five of six fights against Sonny Liston, Joe Frazier, and George Foreman, he proved his superiority over three of the most formidable fighters ever. He is the standard against which supremacy in boxing is measured.

Other men assembled more impressive won-lost records than Ali, fighting and winning more often. But none transcended the sport as he did. If a day were to come—and it won't—when the rest of the world grows tired of adoring Ali, he would still be honored in every boxing gym. Long after he's gone, the dignity and beauty he brought to a brutal profession will be fondly remembered.

Other fighters since Ali have graced the sweet science of boxing and have been great. More great fighters will follow. Someday, as surely as autumn leaves change color and fall to the ground, a young man will step in a boxing ring and be greater than Ali. But Muhammad Ali will always be The Greatest.

★

above EVEN TODAY, ALI IS NEVER FAR FROM A CAMERA.

THE CHAMP IN A REFLECTIVE MOMENT.

MUHAMMAD ALI'S RING RECORD

PROFESSIONAL RECORD: 56 WINS, 5 LOSSES, 37 KOS, 1 KO BY

OLYMPIC RECORD

	Yan Becaus (Belgium)	KO 2
	Genadiy Schatkov (USSR)	W 3
	Tony Madigan (Australia)	W 3
September 5, 1960	Zbigniew Pietrzykowski (Poland)	W 3 (Won Olympic Light-Heavyweight Gold Medal)

PROFESSIONAL FIGHTS

October 29, 1960	Tunney Hunsaker	Louisville, KY	W 6
December 27, 1960	Herb Siler	Miami Beach, FL	KO 4
January 17. 1961	Tony Esperti	Miami Beach, FL	KO 3
February 7, 1961	Jim Robinson	Miami Beach, FL	KO 1
February 21, 1961	Donnie Fleeman	Miami Beach, FL	KO 7
April 19, 1961	Lamar Clark	Louisville, KY	KO 2
June 26, 1961	Duke Sabedong	Las Vegas, NV	W 10
July 22, 1961	Alonzo Johnson	Louisville, KY	W 10
October 7, 1961	Alex Miteff	Louisville, KY	KO 6
November 28, 1961	Willi Besmanoff	Louisville, KY	KO 7
February 19, 1962	Sonny Banks	New York, NY	KO 4
March 28, 1962	Don Warner	Miami Beach, FL	KO 4
April 23, 1962	George Logan	Los Angeles, CA	KO 6

opposite THE NEWLY CROWNED CHAMP TALKING WITH REPORTERS FOLLOWING HIS VICTORY OVER SONNY LISTON. *above* MUHAMMAD ALI LAYING WASTE TO ALL WHO WOULD CHALLENGE HIM: (LEFT TO RIGHT) ARCHIE MOORE, SONNY LISTON, AND FLOYD PATTERSON.

May 19, 1962	Billy Daniels	New York, NY	KO 7
July 20, 1962	Alejandro Lavorante	Los Angeles, CA	KO 5
November 15, 1962	Archie Moore	Los Angeles, CA	KO 4
January 24, 1963	Charlie Powell	Pittsburgh, PA	KO 3
March 13, 1963	Doug Jones	New York, NY	W 10
June 18, 1963	Henry Cooper	London, England	KO 5
February 25, 1964	Sonny Liston	Miami Beach, FL	KO 7 †
May 25, 1965	Sonny Liston	Lewiston, ME	KO 1 ††
November 22, 1965	Floyd Patterson	Las Vegas, NV	KO 12 ††
March 29, 1966	George Chuvalo	Toronto, Canada	W 15 ††
May 21, 1966	Henry Cooper	London, England	KO 6 ††
August 6, 1966	Brian London	London, England	KO 3 ††
September 10, 1966	Karl Mildenberger	Frankfurt, Germany	KO 12 ††
November 14, 1966	Cleveland Williams	Houston, TX	KO 3 ††
February 6, 1967	Ernie Terrell	Houston, TX	W 15 ††
March 22, 1967	Zora Folley	New York, NY	KO 7 ††
October 26, 1970	Jerry Quarry	Atlanta, GA	KO 3
December 7, 1970	Oscar Bonavena	New York, NY	KO 15
March 8, 1971	Joe Frazier	New York, NY	L 15 †††
July 26, 1971	Jimmy Ellis	Houston, TX	KO 12
November 17, 1971	Buster Mathis	Houston, TX	W 12
December 26, 1971	Jurgen Blin	Zurich, Switzerland	KO 7
April 1, 1972	Mac Foster	Tokyo, Japan	W 15
May 1, 1972	George Chuvalo	Vancouver, Canada	W 12
June 27, 1972	Jerry Quarry	Las Vegas, NV	KO 7
July 19, 1972	Al Lewis	Dublin, Ireland	KO 11
September 20, 1972	Floyd Patterson	New York, NY	KO 7
November 21, 1972	Bob Foster	Stateline, NV	KO 8

★

above and opposite **ALI AGAINST (LEFT TO RIGHT) GEORGE CHUVALO, BRIAN LONDON, CLEVELAND WILLIAMS, WILLIAMS AGAIN, CHUCK WEPNER, AND RON LYLE.**

February 14, 1973	Joe Bugner	Las Vegas, NV	W 12
March 31, 1973	Ken Norton	San Diego, CA	L 12
September 10, 1973	Ken Norton	Los Angeles, CA	W 12
October 21, 1973	Rudi Lubbers	Jakarta, Indonesia	W 12
January 28, 1974	Joe Frazier	New York, NY	W 12
October 30, 1974	George Foreman	Kinshasa, Zaire	KO 8 †
March 24, 1975	Chuck Wepner	Cleveland, OH	KO 15 ††
May 16, 1975	Ron Lyle	Las Vegas, NV	KO 11 ††
June 30, 1975	Joe Bugner	Kuala Lumpur, Malaysia	W 15 ††
October 1, 1975	Joe Frazier	Quezon City, Philippines	KO 14 ††
February 20, 1976	Jean-Pierre Coopman	San Juan, PR	KO 5 ††
April 30, 1976	Jimmy Young	Landover, MD	W 15 ††
May 24, 1976	Richard Dunn	Munich, Germany	KO 5 ††
September 28, 1976	Ken Norton	New York, NY	W 15 ††
May 16, 1977	Alfredo Evangelista	Landover, MD	W 15 ††
September 29, 1977	Earnie Shavers	New York, NY	W 15 ††
February 15, 1978	Leon Spinks	Las Vegas, NV	L 15 ††††
September 15, 1978	Leon Spinks	New Orleans, LA	W 15 †
October 2, 1980	Larry Holmes	Las Vegas, NV	KO by 11 †††
December 11, 1981	Trevor Berbick	Nassau, Bahamas	L 10

† Won World Heavyweight Championship
†† Retained World Heavyweight Championship
††† Challenged for World Heavyweight Championship
†††† Lost World Heavyweight Championship

★

ABOUT THE AUTHORS

Thomas Hauser has authored forty books on subjects ranging from boxing to Beethoven. His most celebrated work, *Muhammad Ali: His Life and Times*, was nominated for a Pulitzer Prize and the National Book Award and was honored as the William Hill Sports Book of the Year Award in England. In 2004, Hauser was honored by the Boxing Writers Association of America with the Nat Fleischer Award for Career Excellence in Boxing Journalism. He lives in New York.

Bart Barry is the author of more than 250 articles about the sport of boxing. His work has appeared in 15rounds.com, CBSSports.com, and *The Arizona Republic*. He lives in San Antonio.

ACKNOWLEDGMENTS

I'm indebted to hundreds of people. A special thank you to Jeremy Robson, who appreciates and supports good writing.

—Thomas Hauser

Thank you to Dana Youlin at becker&mayer! for making this book possible. Many thanks to co-author Thomas Hauser for his insights and generosity of spirit. A special thanks to U.B. for remaining sports writing's best reader, and to my father for inspiring an interest in boxing that began with his interest in Muhammad Ali. And finally, deepest gratitude to Pescadita Mia, for whom I write always.

—Bart Barry

page 176 THE GREATEST FIGHTER OF HIS TIME SHARES GYM SPACE WITH THE NEXT GENERATION.

IMAGE CREDITS